The Green Age

Transforming Your Life Choices for the 21st Century

M. Regina Leffers
Director of the Center for the Built Environment
College of Engineering, Technology,
and Computer Science
Indiana University Purdue University Fort Wayne

Matthew Kubik
Associate Professor
College of Engineering, Technology,
and Computer Science
Indiana University Purdue University Fort Wayne

Patrick J. Ashton
Associate Professor
Director of Peace and Conflict Studies
College of Arts and Sciences
Indiana University Purdue University Fort Wayne

Green Age Press
Fort Wayne, Indiana, USA

Green Age Press is an imprint of Create the Green Age LLP.
4750 Parkerdale Drive
Fort Wayne, Indiana 46835-1904

www.thegreenagebook.com

ISBN: 978-0615541280

DEDICATION

We dedicate this book to
the future inhabitants of this planet.
May we make the leap in consciousness
into this Green Age worldview
in time for you to be able to flourish.

Regina's:

For my nephew and niece, Nicholas Leffers and Emily Gore, whose dinner table discussion with me suggested the title for this book. Thanks from Aunt Reg. And for the teachers in my life who have catalyzed a more holistic way of thinking: Teilhard De Chardin, David Bohm, Buckminster Fuller, Paramahansa Yogananda, David Fairchild, Mary Oliver (especially in her poem *Wild Geese*), and for Mac McCaleb.

Matt's:

Dedicated to my visionary teachers, mentors, and friends whose holistic vision truly changed my life: Paul Jaques Grillo, Patrick Horsborough, Kenneth Featherstone, Gerry Foley and John David Mooney. And most of all, to my wife, Sharon, whose efforts at recycling, reuse, and regeneration have fed this sustainable spirit in me. Thank you.

Pat's:

For Bev Purrington, Elizabeth Moon-Gabet, and Risha Swoverland-McLellan, who have facilitated my exploration of the connection between Spirit and Nature; for Fred Buttell who introduced the idea of sustainability early in my intellectual career, and for the great pioneers of the vision of a sustainable society, among them E.F. Schumacker, Jeremy Rifkin, Ernest Callenbach, Robert Rodale. And for Roxy, my partner in a sustainable journey.

CONTENTS

ACKNOWLEDGMENTS

We would like to thank the following people for reading and re-reading our manuscript. They have helped it to become a fine piece of writing. Bobby Nix, Sharon Kubik, Barry Dupen, Daniel Leffers, John and Beth Beams, Randy Roberts, Ann Beeching, Ellen O'Connor Sauers, and Mac McCaleb.

We would also like to thank Barry Dupen for permission to use his photo on the cover of this book.

Visit us at our website: www.createthegreenage.com

THE GREEN AGE

Part One:
The Framework

In Part One we set the framework for the book by explaining what an "Age" is in terms of human life on Earth. While geologists and other scientists talk about ages in the evolution of the planet, we are interested in discussing the ages as they apply to human interaction on and with the Earth over the past 2.5 million years. This is justified for three important reasons: 1) humans have free will and can make conscious choices about their behavior and societal structure; 2) these choices have altered the planet more so than any other species; 3) we are humans writing for other humans, hoping to influence their choices. Thus we will be discussing ages in terms of developments in human societies.

We describe the Hunter-Gatherer Age, approximately the first two-million years of human life and the worldview those human beings must have held. We continue by describing the Agricultural Age which lasted a short time by comparison—just some thousands of years—and its accompanying embedded worldview. Then we human beings moved into the Industrial Age and we've been living in this type of society and utilizing this worldview for approximately the last three hundred years.

Chapter 1:
What is an "Age"?

"It has always been the prime function of mythology and rite to supply the symbols that carry the human spirit forward, in counteraction to those other constant human fantasies that tend to tie it back."[1]

Joseph Campbell

An age is not a specific chronological period, so much as a suite of behavioral and cultural characteristics. The behaviors involve most importantly how humans go about making a living—i.e., producing food, clothing, and shelter and reproducing the next generations. Through collective practice, these behaviors become sedimented (like geological layers of rock) and standardized into institutions that we refer to as the economy, the political system, family and kinship, education, religion, health care. Culture involves the symbolic meaning systems that humans develop and share. It includes material objects and the knowledge of how to use them (technology), values, beliefs, customs, and general knowledge. Values are collective ideas about what is good and desirable. Beliefs are ideas that must be accepted on faith. They are inherently unprovable, yet they inspire and move human behavior.

Culture also includes an embedded worldview (in German, *Weltanschauung*) that flows out of and informs the practices of everyday living. In sociological terms, these practices and their governing principles are called mores (more´ays). Sociologist Robert Bellah and his colleagues observe that "a study of the mores gives us insight into the state of society, its coherence, and its long-term viability. Secondly, it is in the sphere of the mores,

11

and the climates of opinion they express, that we are apt to discern incipient changes of vision—those new flights of the social imagination that may indicate where society is heading."[2] So understanding the mores is crucial to understanding the culture and the worldview that informs it.

As Joseph Campbell has noted, a worldview is essentially mythological, in that it is a sacred narrative that explains the meaning of life in a particular society and provides a prescriptive foundation for that society. A worldview includes three components: (1) cognitive—beliefs about how we got here and where we are going; (2) affective—values that tell us what is important; and (3) evaluative—ethics that point us toward the good. In what follows, we will briefly describe each age in terms of these characteristics.

Humans (the genus *Homo*) have occupied the planet for about 2.4 million years. For tens of thousands of generations the activities of daily living involved hunting, collecting, and preparing food, clothing, and shelter. These early human beings are referred to as Hunter-Gatherers. During that period in our human story, everything that we needed to sustain ourselves was labor intensive. We gathered grains, nuts, seeds, and berries. We had to hunt or fish for any animals we ate. And the hides of the animals we ate became our clothing and shelter.

Furthermore, we made all of the tools we used for hunting, food preparation, and clothes-making. We didn't live in one place. We followed our food and water; we moved with the animals, the bounty of the land, the rivers, lakes, and streams. We didn't think of the land as something that was ours, but rather, both a gift and something of which we were a part.

Our societies were small in scale, usually consisting of two to four dozen people. The members were tied closely to one another, and to the natural environment. Culture and daily living were seamlessly integrated. The belief system of people in these societies is called animism. We believed that spirits inhabit everything in the world, from inanimate objects to people. We prayed and subsequently gave thanks for a successful hunt and a bountiful gathering. Shamans, who mediated between the spirit and the natural world, led various magic rituals. Although investigators can't know for sure, it appears that these societies highly valued the feminine, particularly the female as a symbol of fertility. Indeed, some of the earliest artifacts we have from these societies are so-called "Venus" figurines. The one pictured below was carved 25,000 years ago.[3]

While there is some debate about whether these societies were truly matriarchal, there is little doubt that they were fundamentally egalitarian.[4] In Hunter-Gatherer societies every member of the group is important. The success of the group—whether it was hunting and gathering, decision-making, or reproduction—depended on the contribution of each member. Thus ethics, or the good, was that which contributed above all to the survival of the group.

The transition from the Age of Hunter-Gatherers to the Agricultural Age took thousands of years. The Agricultural Age began with the practice of horticulture, in which gardens were created by cutting down vegetation and burning it to create fertile soil. This practice of slash-and-burn cultivation, as it was known, was necessitated by the growth of human population and the depletion of large game through intensive hunting. We began by staying close to a water source, and saving some of the grains and seeds that we gathered for planting.

As we no longer had to move significant distances in search of food, our settlements became more permanent and we began to accumulate more possessions. Our settlements became larger and denser, typically 150-200 members, but in some cases as large as several thousand. While each community was generally self-sufficient, trade with other communities brought in new resources. Our tools became more and more sophisticated as we learned how to obtain and work various metals. Since villages now had territory to protect, physically violent confrontations with other groups began to develop as a regular occurrence.

The values of horticultural society emphasized the mutual obligations of kinship. This included our ancestors, who had lived and worked in the same place and were buried nearby. We believed that they now inhabited a supernatural realm which was seamlessly integrated with the realm of the natural. We believed the ancestors could still influence events in the natural world, and we implored them to do so.

The invention of the plow led to full-scale agriculture and intensive cultivation. The domestication of animals provided meat, milk, and fertilizer. The creation of a surplus of food made possible significant population growth and craft specialization. But it also led to inequality as first religious then secular political leaders captured control of the surplus. This development—what anthropologist William Ury calls "locking up the food"—was associated with the rise of a class system and the state. War became increasingly systematic and violent.

In truth, however, the violence and domination we have known are the product not so much of human nature but the complex logic of settling down, intensive reliance on land, population increase, the weakening of the third side [third parties who could mediate disputes], the closing of the exit option, the development of authoritarian hierarchies, the growth of the state, and the contagion of war. At the bottom of this logic is the dependence on fixed-pie resources—first of land and then of power over other human beings."[5]

The Agricultural Age is also associated with the rise of civilization—i.e., living in cities. But the cities of this period had an organic connection to the land. For the most part they had sustainable populations. The dominant myth developed into theism—both polytheism, in which capricious gods played sport with humans, or monotheism, in which god was a demanding and punitive patriarch (e.g., the Pharaoh, the Hebrew god of the Old Testament). The ethics of the Agricultural Age involved ethnocentrism, in which "our" group had to be protected from "them." This was often accomplished through war and ruthless, violent practices like headhunting, cannibalism, human sacrifice, and slavery.

The next transition—from the Agricultural Age to the Industrial Age—took just some hundreds, rather than thousands, of years. The Industrial Age began with changes in the way people lived and worked. Increased global exploration and trade led to new resources and markets. Factories were developed as engines of profit. In an effort to rationalize production and direct and control the laborers, tools and production processes were mechanized.[6] While natural sources of energy like water power were used initially, as mechanization proceeded it increasingly relied upon non-renewable resources—first coal and then petroleum. As landowners turned from farming to grazing, the rural population was forced off the land and into cities, which now grew far beyond the ability of the local economy to sustain them. Instead of working the land, we began working in factories. Rather than growing our own food, we built machines and bought food. During this Age, agriculture has become a mechanical and chemical process that is primarily orchestrated by large agribusinesses utilizing huge, energy-intensive machines. It is an extension of the factory process.

The advent of this age was not entirely negative, of course. The Industrial Age, for instance, extended individual freedom. Freed from the traditional village, in the cities humans created new cultural practices. Urban consumers created a mass market for products. Goods that were formerly luxuries were now available on a mass scale. Large-scale political movements extended human rights. In the face of this new emphasis on individual self-determination (economically, politically, socially) the accompanying myth was of a personal and benevolent god (e.g., the Christian god of the New Testament).

In the Industrial Age, practices of farming that nourish the soil have been replaced by chemical enhancements. Everything from seeds to beef cattle are being injected with growth hormones and anti-something chemicals (e.g. antibiotics, pesticides, and antibacterial serums). And we know how our diets have changed! We eat mainly processed "foods" that are laced with preservatives, and come mostly from somewhere else on Earth, and not from where we live. Just check the origin label on the fruits available at your local grocery store the next time you purchase, and think about how much fossil fuel went into transporting this fruit from its country or State of origin. At this point in time, we are coming to understand that the way in which we've been living is not sustainable. If we continue along this path of failing to nourish the earth, the "mess" that our grandchildren will inherit will be unable to support human life. We have to change and the change has to be speedy. In fact, this transition from the Industrial Age to the Sustainable, or Green Age, must take just decades.

The associated myth of the Green Age is transcendental idealism, which is a belief, not in a god or gods, but in a set of sacred principles of thought and conduct. Principles like Gaia— the notion of a living earth[7]—spiritual humanism, and new age mysticism emphasize the evolution of human consciousness and a harmonious relationship to each other and our natural environment. Rather than domination—of the earth and each other—the emphasis will be on the feminine principles of nurturance and connection. The ethics of the Green Age, as we will see later in this book, revolve around community, personal and collective responsibility, and sustainability.[8]

So, how can we do that? How can we make the change from the Industrial Age to the Green Age in just a few years? That is the "million-dollar-question" that we will attempt to answer in this book. We believe that it is possible, but we also understand the complexity of the task at hand. Our way of living, all of the choices we make, all of our habits and preferences are supported by an underlying value and belief system that is largely unconscious. This is the "life-soup" of which our worldview consists. Our worldview provides the unconscious assumptions, values, and imperatives from which we make automatic choices in life. The living habits and practices of our culture set the framework that establishes a worldview. By identifying the underlying beliefs and values that are unconsciously held inside of the Industrial Age worldview, and suggesting the beliefs and values of which a Green Age worldview would consist, individually, we can more easily and rapidly make the needed internal replacement.

When we make conscious that which is unconscious, we are taking the first step toward change. This change will involve (as a minimum) our relationship with nature, resources and how we make things, patterns of consumption, usage of energy, the way in which we educate, how we grow our food, and the way in which we build the structures for our use. Using this rubric, we uncover some guidelines for transforming the predominant Industrial Age mechanical world view to one that will ultimately be more aligned with a sustainable future.

Part Two:
The Industrial Age

In Part Two we explain the worldview contained in the Industrial Age. The values and beliefs that are embedded in this worldview are the ones from which we make our everyday choices. This is the worldview into which every human being who is alive today was born. Because of this, the values and beliefs from which we make choices are hidden from our conscious mind—they are automatic and therefore, unexamined for their worthiness. We bring them to the surface so they may be examined and decisions made about them: do we keep them, or lose them? Are they worthy of moving into the future with us; or are they unworthy values and beliefs that must be discarded (like a worn out pair of running shoes)?

Chapter 2:
The Industrial Age In A Gearbox
(instead of "in a nutshell")!

The Industrial Age is the one in which we've been living for about 300 years. Modern philosopher Henryk Skolimowski identified the dominant worldview of our era as *Mechanos*.[9] In this view, the universe is seen as a giant machine, whose operation is mechanical and predictable, and which can by understood through the analysis of its individual component parts. The *Mechanos* worldview was developed at the beginning of the Industrial Age by philosophers such as Francis Bacon, René Descartes, and Isaac Newton and it has provided a framework for our cultural values, beliefs, choices and actions throughout this age.

Francis Bacon is the philosopher who came up with the standard scientific method of acquiring knowledge that we've all learned (and still teach) in our fifth grade science class.[10] In this view, we think of ourselves as being separate and objective observers, able to study something from a detached and disinterested standpoint, and able to come away from the experience with knowledge about whatever we've observed. Intuitive, holistic, and engaged analysis is discouraged.

René Descartes is the philosopher who most famously said, "I think; therefore, I am," and most of us have first encountered its Latin version: "Cogito, ergo sum." That statement became a cornerstone of Western philosophy and thought—and is the idea to which most philosophers have responded since that time. In putting forth the idea that "I think; therefore, I am," Descartes originated the separation of mind and body in Western thought and culture. He conceived of nature as essentially a machine which can be rationally controlled. In the words of Descartes, humans are "masters and possessors of nature."[11]

Isaac Newton was the scientist who established the physical laws formulating the Mechanical world view.[12] We've applied these laws to our physical world, and we can see that they have a scope of application. However, these ideas also underlie the desire that we have in Western culture to apply them to human relationships and organizations. We thought that if we could just use them to order the inherently messy quality of human beings living and working together (those dratted emotions), we could make them ordered and predictable.

The *Mechanos* dualistic relationship of humans to the natural world is amplified in the economic theories of Adam Smith and the political theory of John Locke. The 17th century English philosopher John Locke wrote: "The negation of nature is the way toward Happiness."[13] Locke argued that people must be "emancipated from the bonds of nature." Locke also preached unlimited economic growth where a harmonious society depended upon the amassing of individual wealth.

Adam Smith, the 18th century father of modern economics, believed that self interest was also of social benefit so that an individual "by pursuing his own interest, frequently promotes that of the society more effectually than when he intends to promote it."[14] The pursuit of self interest, without consequence, expanded to the scale of the industrial revolution has led to our current environmental degradation.

We summarize the *Mechanos* worldview as follows:

- Nature is to be dominated by humans as a divine right and resources are endless.

- Growth is necessary.

- Progress is amassing material abundance.

- Competition is a requirement for human advancement.

- Rationality, Logic, and Scientific Method are superior to Nature and Intuition.[15]

One of the common cartoon images of our culture is that of the young man arriving on the mountain top to ask an ascetic wise man for the secret of the universe. As with most pithy questions, the answer is usually already at hand, if we can only wake up and look around. And as with most prophets, the answers that are at hand are generally ignored.

Frederick Soddy (1877–1956) was an English radio-chemist who received the Nobel Prize for Chemistry in 1921, and has a crater named for him on the far side of the moon. It was Soddy's work in radioactive elements that eventually led to the development of one of our most powerful methods of domination over nature—the atomic bomb. Later in his career Soddy turned his attention to the role of energy in economic systems. Like the wise guru, Soddy identifies the secret of the universe:

> The Laws of Thermodynamics control in the last resort the rise and fall of political systems, the freedom or bondage of Nations, the movements of commerce and industry, the origins of wealth and poverty and the general physical welfare of the race.[16]

WHAT? In science class we learned that the laws of thermodynamics were mostly about mechanical engineering. Rudolf Clausius (1822-1888) first laid out the basic ideas of the Second Law of Thermodynamics in his 1850 paper, *On the mechanical theory of heat.[17]* Clausius' definition of the Second Law of Thermodynamics is stated in terms of the mechanical worldview. "No machine whose working fluid undergoes a cycle can absorb heat from one system, reject heat to another system and produce no other effect." But Soddy had a bigger vision.

Like most great truths, the Laws of Thermodynamics seem complicated, but once explained are disarmingly simple and obvious. Like the photograph of the Earth when looked at from space, they have enormous consequences. The First Law is the "conservation law." It says that energy cannot be created or destroyed; only its form can change, but not its essence. In other words, what is…is. It's all you get and you're not getting any more. However, there's a catch.

There are many versions of the Second Law of Thermodynamics, more simply stated than Clausius' version. Ultimately, they all have the same meaning, which is to explain the phenomenon of irreversibility in nature. In simple terms, the second law is an expression of the fact that over time energy concentrations inevitably, relentlessly move from maximum potential to full depletion.

This is easy to visualize with a mechanical model. Fill a thermos bottle with hot soup for lunch. With the lid on you have a maximum concentration of energy. However, if you forget to eat the soup and don't open it until the next day you would find the temperature of the liquid to be the same as the room in which it was left. Even though we did all we could to create a heat retaining jar to retard the flow of energy, it passed through the thermos walls until the concentrated energy reached a state of equilibrium with its surroundings.

The universe craves equilibrium. We might say that maximum potential energy represents order. It is the essence of nature that all systems will move from order toward disorder. In some examples the movement from concentrated energy/order is quick, and explosive. Light the wick of a Molotov cocktail and the transfer of energy from available to unavailable is fairly immediate. And it's irreversible.

The measure of irreversibility is called entropy. The Second Law of Thermodynamics is also an expression of the universal law of increasing entropy. This law states that the entropy of a system which is not in equilibrium will tend to increase over time, approaching a maximum value at equilibrium. Another way of thinking about entropy is that it is the amount of energy that is no longer available for purposes useful for humans or what we call "work". As pointed out by author Jeremy Rifkin, "In fact pollution is the sum total of all the available energy in the world that has been transformed into unavailable energy."[18] Pollution is therefore is just another name for entropy.

Ecology is the study of natural interacting communities. A simple ecosystem model would include an outside energy input from the sun and a food chain of plants, plant eaters, and meat eaters. As each life form dies it is in turn "eaten" by bacteria and other digesters returning the remaining nutrients into the system. As energy transfers from one living entity in the system to another, a small amount of energy is given off as heat which is no longer available and cannot be recovered. In most natural systems the measure of entropy is actually rather small.

Taken from a global point of view, entropy is actually an inverse relationship with the amount of resources left for us to use. Increasing entropy is not a good thing. If an alarm clock is wound and starts running down it represents potential energy moving toward energy equilibrium. Entropy is a measure of how far along this evening-out process has progressed—how much the spring has unwound. What is left over is how much time is left on the clock.

M. King Hubbert (1903–1989) was a geoscientist who worked at the Shell Research Laboratory in Houston, Texas. He made several important contributions to geology, geophysics, and petroleum geology, most notably the Hubbert peak theory. This theory has important social and political ramifications. Hubbert is most well-known for his studies on the capacities of oil fields and natural gas reserves. He predicted that, for any given geographical area (from an individual oil field to the planet as a whole) the rate of petroleum production of the reserve over time would resemble a bell curve.[19] (See the graph on the next page.)

Hubbert presented a paper, based on this theory, to the 1956 meeting of the American Petroleum Institute in San Antonio, Texas, which predicted that overall petroleum production would peak in the United States between the late 1960s and the early 1970s. At first his prediction received much criticism. Earlier predictions of oil capacity had been made over the preceding half century, but these had been based purely on reserve and production data rather than on past discovery trends, and proved to be false. In 1970 Hubbert's prediction proved correct. A look at a recent projection of Hubbert's bell curve for world energy production indicates a peak between 2006 and 2010. After this time petroleum production will decrease and prices are projected to rise rapidly.

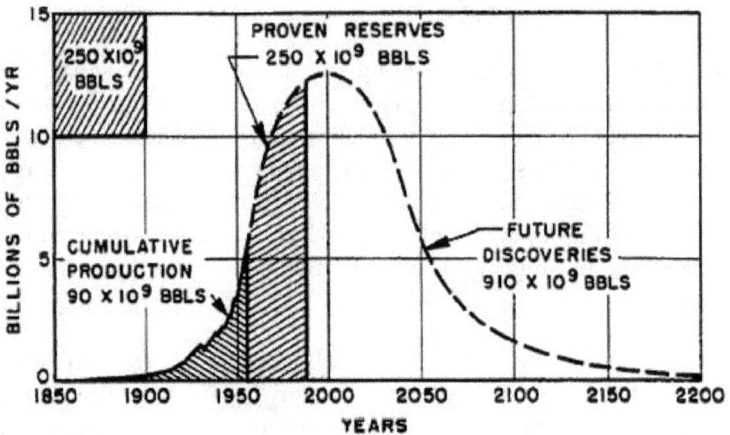

The Greek myth of Pandora can be read as a metaphor for the Second Law of Thermodynamics, the entropy law and perhaps our Industrial Age. Pandora, which in Greek means "giver of all, all-endowed," had been given a gift of a large jar which was full. Zeus instructed her to keep it closed, but she had also been given the gift of curiosity, and ultimately opened it. When she opened it, all of the evils, ills, diseases, and burdensome labor that mankind had not known previously, escaped from the jar, and could not be put back inside. However, it is said, that at the very bottom of the container, there lay Hope. Our hope resides in rapidly moving toward the Green Age.

In 1926 Frederick Soddy wrote *Wealth, Virtual Wealth and Debt: The Solution of the Economic Paradox*, a book that presaged the market crash of 1929 and equally applies to the economic woes of the 21st Century. Soddy pointed out the fundamental difference between real wealth, like buildings, machinery, oil, pigs, and virtual wealth, in the form of money and debt. (To this we might add all the ephemeral wealth held in "investments" where value is only based on the accumulated faith and trust of society—i.e. electronic statements.) Soddy wrote that real wealth is subject to the inescapable entropy law of thermodynamics and would rot, rust, or wear out with age; while money and debt, what we are calling ephemeral wealth, are accounting devices invented by humans. They are subject only to the laws of mathematics, which are subject to all kinds of manipulation. Just ask Bernie Madoff.

Rather than decaying, virtual wealth, in the form of debt, compounding at the current rate of interest actually grows without bounds. In his book Soddy used concrete examples to demonstrate what he considered this flaw in money economics such as this: A farmer who raises pigs faces biophysical limits on how many pigs he can take to market. But if that pig farmer took on debt, along with its accompanying promise to repay at a future date, he would in effect be issuing a claim or lien on his future production of pigs. If he borrowed the equivalent value of 100 pigs, he could represent the loan on his balance sheet as "-100 pigs."

While debt as the farmer's accounting entry is negative, negative pigs do not really exist. If the farmer should suffer a series of lean years and be unable to pay the interest, he might soon owe more pigs than could be raised on his farm. After a year, with interest looming, he might show "-110 pigs," in 5 years, "-161 pigs," in 40 (assuming a patient bank), "-4526 pigs." When the bank finally comes to call on the pig farmer to collect repayment of its loan, it could well find that most of the virtual wealth that had grown so appealingly on its books had to be written off as a loss. Soddy remains the unheard prophet

Monetary systems have historically been based on some form of physical element—usually gold. Nobel Prize-winning economist Paul Krugman describes it this way, "The legend of King Midas has been generally misunderstood. Most people think the curse that turned everything the old miser touched into gold, leaving him unable to eat or drink, was a lesson in the perils of avarice. But Midas' true sin was his failure to understand monetary economics. What the gods were really telling him is that gold is just a metal. If it sometimes seems to be more, that is only because society has found it convenient to use gold as a medium of exchange—a bridge between other, truly desirable, objects."[20]

Since the 1970s the American monetary system is not backed by any physical commodity. In fact, as Krugman points out, "the Federal Reserve is not obliged to tie the dollar to anything. It can print as much or as little money as it deems appropriate. There are powerful advantages to such an unconstrained system. Above all, the Fed is free to respond to actual or threatened recessions by pumping in money."[21] This is known as a fiat money system where the only thing that gives the money value is its relative scarcity and the faith placed in it by the people that use it. As we recognize the interconnections of a world economy, Krugman notes, "modern nations have chosen, with reasonable justification, to renounce their monetary autonomy in favor of some external standard, the standard they choose these days is always the currency of another, presumably more responsible, nation."[22]

Unfortunately, History shows us that fiat money systems have a flaw. Hyper-inflation is the terminal stage of any fiat currency. In hyper-inflation, money loses most of its value practically overnight. Hyper-inflation is often the result of increasing regular inflation to the point where all confidence in money is lost. In a fiat monetary system, the value of money is based on confidence, and once that confidence is gone, money irreversibly becomes worthless, regardless of its scarcity. Gold has replaced every fiat currency for the past 3000 years. Krugman advises us not to commit the sin of King Midas. We must remember "that gold is only a metal, and that its value comes only from the truly useful goods for which it can be exchanged."[23]

In other words, exchanged for real wealth (buildings, machinery, and pigs) as Soddy explained. And real wealth is tied to energy availability. Whether we are paying with gold or with a piece of paper representing our collective good faith in its value, what we do know is that in the Industrial Age we are not paying for the true cost of our consumables. First of all, the word consumable is a bit of a joke. What we know from the laws of thermodynamics is that nothing is ever consumed. An objects form is simply changed with some amount of energy lost (entropy) in the process.

What we are not paying for in the Industrial Age is the cost of environmental damage, social inequity, and personal isolation that our high energy oil culture has created. Someone else (our descendants) will be paying for the problems we are creating today—the problems that are impacting the health of our planet. due to our unrelenting growth and inefficient use of resources.

M. King Hubbert believed that the growth value that we hold is a cultural constraint. During the last two-hundred years, we've built exponential growth into both our culture and our economy, and our stability in both systems is dependent on that level of growth. He believed that we aren't able to deal with problems in our society or economy from a perspective that doesn't entail confronting growth as a central component of the solution.[24] Insofar as economic growth is driven by oil consumption growth, it will be the task of those of us living in the age of decreasing oil availability to creatively face significant economic, environmental and social challenges of the future. Bob Dylan's anthem of social change seems strangely prophetic when applied to the coming age of oil scarcity. Surely,

> "The order is
> Rapidly fadin'
> And the first one now
> Will later be last
> For the times they are a-changin'."[25]

Chapter 3:
The Industrial Age Worldview

Philosophers throughout time have maintained "that we confer value onto that which we choose by the act of our choosing….We are the only biological beings in nature who have both the ability to choose and the ability to be conscious of the choices we make. Whether that choice is expressed and acted on through our thoughts, our feelings, or our actions, it is the composite of these choices that are the details of who we are as well as who we are becoming."[26] The fact that we are the only biological beings on the planet who are able to make conscious choices about what we value, believe, and do means that we are the only ones who can actually perform the function of stewardship. If the Earth and its inhabitants are to flourish and thrive, we must think about and align our values, beliefs, and our doings so they will actually produce that outcome.

A couple of obvious ways that we can look for the values in a society are to examine what choices we make and what we mean when we use the word, "progress." When we "make progress" we feel we've moved in a positive direction toward something desirable. So we can look at what has grown and developed—what actually continues to exist and thrive in society to find out what it is that we value.

In the early 20th century German sociologist Max Weber referred to the increasing rationalization and bureaucratization of society as an "iron cage" that we were constructing for ourselves.[27] George Ritzer updated this thesis by referring to the process as *McDonaldization*.[28] Epitomized by the familiar and monotonous similarity of the fast food chain, the process aims to spread the values of *efficiency*, *predictability*, *calculability*, and *control* to a wide variety of goods and services, from hotels and restaurants to education and health care.

Efficiency in this model means the minimization of time and distance. At McDonald's the goal is to process the food and the customers in the least amount of time possible with the fewest steps. (It is, after all, marketed as *fast* food!) Large pictures and the numbering of menu items reduce the time it takes to order. The expectation that customers will fill their own drinks and get their own napkins and condiments reduces serving time as well as the number of employees needed. The business plan involves locating multiple restaurants in various high-traffic locations so that customers can easily access them.

Predictability means that customers can rely on the fact that the product is identical over time and at all locales. No matter where you go in the United States or around the world, a Big Mac and fries will look and taste the same. It may not be gourmet food, but it is routinely identical. Moreover, limited menu choices reduce the number of items needed, make ordering and inventory control more predictable, and reduce employee discretion. Predictability also means that employee behavior is scripted so that the interaction with each customer and at each location conforms to a consistent corporate standard. ("Would you like fries with that?") Today, even the initial greeting in the drive-thru is recorded to eliminate any departures from the approved script.

Calculability refers to the quantification of every aspect of the production and delivery of a product or service. In a fast food restaurant, each food element is carefully measured to control costs and increase profits. Customers are encouraged to calculate the value in upsizing or "supersizing" their order. At the same time, a "value menu" increases volume at the lower-cost end of the menu.

Customers as well as employees are tightly controlled in the McDonald's model. The entire food ordering, production, and delivery process is automated to the greatest degree possible. The technology as well as company rules rigidly regulates employee behavior. Customer choices are limited in the interests of efficiency and profits. Franchisees must rigidly follow corporate policy.

Ritzer and others show that, in the Industrial Age, the McDonald's model has spread, not only throughout the food industry, but to housing ("McMansions"), shopping (malls), lodging (hotel chains), tourism (Disney World, cruise ships), relationships ("speed dating," internet matchmaking), education (charter schools, preoccupation with test scores, rating colleges), and health care ("Docs in a Box"), among other industries.

In the Industrial Age, the overwhelming emphasis on consumption as self-fulfillment results in what Ritzer calls a "disenchantment" with the world. Ironically, efforts to re-enchant the world through the construction of "cathedrals of consumption" within extensive "landscapes of consumption" has the effect of producing further disenchantment, disillusion, and disconnection among individuals and communities.[29]

The Industrial Age also values *locomotion, speed, precision, accuracy, distance, and hyper-efficiency*. When we think about commercials that attempt to sell cars, we discover that these are cultural values that car manufacturers believe will successfully get us to buy today. If we can afford them, we buy cars—preferably one car for every family member who is of driving age. And we like our cars to go fast—from zero to sixty miles per hour in six seconds! Imagine the general reaction to a sales pitch that touted a car that would go from zero to sixty mph in six minutes!

We also value that which is *short-term* and *disposable*. We can see this in the amounts of trash that we throw away, recycle, or compost each day. We can look at our dumps and dumpsters, our landfills-turned-mountains, created with grass-covered garbage that produces methane (and other) gases, in order to get a good glimpse of these values in action.

We value *expediency*. Whatever we do, whatever gets done for us, wherever we go, we want it to happen fast—preferably yesterday! Taking time is something that we must make ourselves do when we're on vacation. But, of course, we've travelled to our vacation destination by jet so that we could begin relaxing just as fast as we possibly can. We impatiently drive behind "slow-pokes," honk at them as we pass them, sometimes giving them a "salute" to criticize their un-hurried driving. Even though we may fantasize about a slower way of life (from a bygone era) we all recognize ourselves as participants at some level in this frenetic way of living.

We value *conquest, colonizing, expansion,* the concept of *survival of the fittest,* and *having no limits.* We can see these values writ large in all of our organizations, whether governments, religions, businesses, or games. We've made conquests of lands and peoples by making war, movies, jeans, and hamburgers. We've colonized and expanded by sending people to other cities or countries—to spread the word as missionaries, to spread our country's boundaries as settlers, or to expand our businesses by sending people to sell our goods.

We also value things that run themselves. This value is easily visible in the progression of the way that cars have developed. We've gone from hand-cranked cars, to cars that can be started by pressing a button from inside the house, and from manual transmissions to cars that automatically shift gears themselves. We can see it in our appliances when we look at the new vacuums that just get turned on and proceed to move around the floor in a self-propelled, dirt-sucking frenzy. Our washing machines have gone from washboards and tubs that involved hands-on hard labor, to wringer washers in which each article was hand fed through the rollers that would wring the water out, to automatic washers requiring only that we put things in and remove them when the work of cleaning is done.

We also value the combination of "short-term fixes" with "expediency" and the value that perceives "human labor as demeaning." One example that illustrates this powerfully is in the way we treat our own bodies. Most of us take medicine instead of making the daily life changes needed that would correct the problem. The following example is extreme, but we'll probably recognize ourselves in the behavior to a lesser degree.

Regina's Story

A friend that I have known for many years has a variety of physical problems and takes about thirty different medicines aimed at addressing them. A couple of the problems are that he is overweight, has high-blood pressure, and adult onset diabetes. I asked him if he thought he could begin walking a little each day to reduce the physical problems. His reply was that his doctor had just gotten all of his medicine "right," so they were working together. He didn't want to change anything he was doing because the way in which his medicine worked together would be compromised! He didn't consider that if he would just exercise a little each day, the activity would probably solve many of his health problems and the medicine might be able to be reduced or eliminated.

I also have an example that is extreme in the opposite direction. Another long-time friend who was also overweight was diagnosed with diabetes. He became aware that something was seriously wrong one weekend when he was in the middle of conducting a three-day seminar. His doctor diagnosed the problem and immediately started treatment with the medicine remedy, insulin. He started an exercise program for himself that very day—walking—and within a matter of weeks, he was running. He also eliminated sugary sweets. Within a month of living in this new way, he was back at the doctor's office and his body tested as being completely clear of diabetes. That was a number of years ago. He has maintained this new way of living, and his body remains free of diabetes. Both of the people I've described here are now in their early sixties. One walks with a cane and is in very poor health; the other runs every day and is in vibrant health.

In the Industrial Age we produce material goods non-stop. We work three shifts, around the clock, seven days a week. We work overtime, earning time-and-a-half, or double-time. We accumulate material goods non-stop. We "keep up with the Jones's," and hold to the old saying that "those with the most toys win." As we consume material goods non-stop, we "shop until we drop," or reward ourselves with "shopping sprees."

Plastic storage boxes hold the proof of our amassed goods. Now available with orange lids, they are sold in November so that we can pack and store our Halloween decorations and costumes. Then we pull out our green and red plastic storage boxes (which we've previously purchased on the post-Holiday shelves at the supermarkets and box stores) to retrieve our Christmas trees, decorations, and lights for the season. We could also find evidence of our belief in the value of material abundance in most of our attics, basements, closets, and garages We can find it in our dish cupboards, on our book shelves, in DVD cabinets, telephone jacks, and cable hookups.

We believe that time—measured by the rotation of planets – has value equivalent to material goods. "Time is Money" is an adage that rules many lives. Efficiency is gauged by the stopwatch, regardless of the "over engineering" that it takes to achieve the results. Our cars are powered so that we can zoom away from stop lights even though they consume a majority of their fuel in acceleration. Mechanical heating systems are oversized to meet the most extreme condition that rarely occurs instead of the average climatic conditions. Our groveling to the god of Time is obsequious devotion to a false idol. It is a human construct.

We believe in our right to own property, and most of us act on that belief. We own our homes, and sometimes own second and third homes that we use occasionally for rest and relaxation. We obviously believe in the value of the Scientific Method of gaining knowledge, because that is what we continue to use in academic research and we continue to teach it as a valid method of knowledge acquisition to students. We believe that predictability is best—we want to know what is going to happen, probably because of issues of safety and preparedness.

We seem to believe in permanent material growth, and that there is an endless supply of natural resources that will allow the material growth to continue forever. Many of us believe that the more we make individually, the more society benefits collectively. Money automatically gets extracted from our payroll checks and is put into the Federal, State, and local tax funds that provide our society's infrastructure. Other monies go into a general fund for Medicare, Medicaid, and Social Security.

We may also have automatic donations removed from our payroll checks that go into the United Way general fund to assist those in society who have needs that go unmet. We tithe. We very likely make contributions to our favorite charities. We believe that each individual operating with their own best interests in mind (with little consideration for the best interests of the collective) will allow scarcity to be overcome by surplus.

Do we believe that change is bad? We seem to resist change with all our might, wait until the last possible minute, and then, finally, make the change that is needed. On an individual scale, we don't: stop smoking, start exercising, reduce our weight, take action to reduce stress, or start weaving play into our everyday lives until we get a health scare of some sort. On a large scale, when we knew at least a year in advance that a hurricane could destroy much of New Orleans, we failed to act and make the changes necessary to protect the city.

On a societal scale, we continue to make financial decisions for our public buildings based on low up-front costs, even though we know that it means the costs of operating the building will be staggering. On a planetary scale, we continue to produce massive amounts of greenhouse gases, though we know they are contributing to accelerating and perhaps irreversible global warming. Our concern is for today.

Thomas Friedman provides a penetrating critique of this phenomenon in his book *Hot, Flat, and Crowded*. "The destabilization of both the Market and Mother Nature had the same root causes," he says. "That is why Bear Stearns and the polar bears both faced extinction at the same time. That is why Citibank, Iceland's banks, and the ice banks of Antarctica all melted down at the same time. The same recklessness undermined all of them."[30]

One of the principal beliefs embedded in our current worldview—a legacy of the Enlightenment—sees History as a progressive journey from societal confusion and disorder to a measured, predictable world order. Surely this must be true if we can overpower the bondage of gravity by blasting off into space in order to take planetary self portraits. Surely this must be true as we entertain ourselves with microchip marvel toys and gird the earth in bands of concrete highway to help speed us from one place to another. Unfortunately all this "order" comes at a price.

We believe that science and technology will solve all of our problems. We see technology as a transformer because it takes energy from nature and changes it into human culture. We also believe that technology and nature are independent and unconnected. We see progress in taking the less-ordered natural world and harnessing it to create a more ordered material environment for ourselves. We believe that we are creating greater value out of the natural world than is inherent in its original state.

We do our best to control, conquer, manipulate, and exploit nature. We build dikes to hold the ocean back so that we can build homes and buildings. And when the ocean breaches the dike and destroys the homes (as it most surely will), we rebuild the dike and rebuild the homes in exactly the same place. We change the course of streams, making them turn right-angled corners around business parks and streets. Then when a large weather event happens and the water refuses to turn the corner and floods the homes downstream, we are shocked and chagrined. But we don't correct it.

In the Industrial Age Worldview, we believe that manual labor is demeaning. All we have to do is look to our pay scales to find evidence of this belief. In general, the harder the physical labor, the lower the wage. During the first half of the 1900s, we had to form unions to make companies pay a living wage to laborers. In manufacturing, production has become increasingly automated and standardized, taking creativity and individual decision making away from the folks who provide the labor in a production line. In fact, human labor is now just another aspect of the line assembly. We clock in and we clock out. We "*have to* go to work." If we provide manual labor, the idea of work itself has become a burden, even in our own minds.

We can also look to our food production to see our beliefs in the value of technology-as-solution and manual labor-as-demeaning. Our food used to be grown locally by small, family-owned farms. They rotated the crops and grazing animals in the fields in order to give nourishment back to the soil. The rotation went something like this: after the crop is harvested from the field, beef cattle are moved in to the field to graze on the stover (the plant material left behind after harvest).

After the beeves have left enough droppings, flies have laid eggs on it, and fly larvae have hatched, the beeves are moved to the next field and the chicken tractor is set in place. The chickens have plenty of food in the larvae and they also leave their nutrient gift for the soil, in the form of their droppings. By the time the chickens are moved out of the field, the soil has been so replenished that the next crop planted is chock full of the kinds of vitamins and minerals that we human beings need to ingest from the food that we grow and eat.

Instead of these organic, local, family-owned farms, we now have huge agri-business owned mega-farms and chemical-geneticized farming. Con-Agra is the largest example of these businesses in the United States. It is a centralized farming business that uses approximately 18,400 BTU's of energy to produce one dollar of output. The yield per acre is roughly the same as the small, organic farm described in the paragraph above; however, transporting the grain or produce from the centralized location across the country to distribution centers, and/or supermarkets elevates the cost dramatically in terms of energy.

And finally, we believe that death is evil and that life must be a constant war against it. Since we believe that we are both separate from the Earth and that we have dominion (interpreted with dominating behavior rather than steward behavior) over it, we are clearly not "of" the Earth. We have created an entire industry to shield us from death. Bodies are not "dead" they are "remains." Chemically transfused, waxed and hermitically wrapped—we do everything we can to protect ourselves from this natural flow of energy.

Part Three: Where We Are Now

In Part Three, we explain where we are now by telling the story of Matt's family journey. The story of his family is a good illustration of the transition we human beings have made from the Agricultural to the Industrial Age worldviews and from there into the Green Age worldview as we follow Matt's grandfather's journey to "the new world," and his labor change from farming to industry. Then we follow Matt's father, determined to erase his European peasant roots through his work achievements, perfect lawn, and status cars. And finally, we end with Matt himself, a man determined to recover a sense of connection with the Earth and do what he can to preserve it for future generations.

Chapter 4:
The Bewildering Space between the Ages

Matt's Story

My father, born in 1911, grew up living what today we would call a "green" lifestyle. There was almost no waste. If a pig was slaughtered almost all of it was used. Fuel was local and usually a renewable resource. My grandfather was a creative and resourceful man who made much of what his family needed. Almost all necessary commerce was local or within easy reach in a nearby town via public transportation. The neighbors were mutually supportive and the size of the urban area was essentially sustainable through local resources. His "peasant village", as he used to call it, was near the Russian border in what is now Slovakia. My father didn't know he was "green" and he didn't particularly want to be "green."

When my father was sixteen my grandfather moved the family as part of the great Eastern European migration to America. America! It was the land of limitless opportunity and endless resources. In the early 1920s no one questioned that growth was inevitable or that it might be less than desirable. (Few question that premise today.) They moved to an industrial city on the edge of Lake Michigan where the largest sand dune on the lower shores, the Hoosier Slide, was systematically being hauled away to make glass. It was replaced with a coal-fired electricity generating plant. My grandfather spent the rest of his working life as a bricklayer in the furnaces of the local factory that manufactured railroad cars.

I don't know that my grandfather believed that his life was an advancement from a lesser existence to one that was more beneficial. I believe that life was meager in Slovakia and was probably fairly meager in the U.S. when he arrived, on the brink of the 1930s depression. My grandfather was somewhat religious

43

and probably believed literally in the biblical command of Genesis 1:26, which gave man *dominion* over the animals and told him to *subdue* the earth. It was pretty much understood that God gave man free rein to do anything he wants to the earth for his own benefit. Because of that, we just got on with moving that sand and building those railroad cars.

My father's life, on the other hand, was a lifelong struggle to make the journey from what he saw as societal degradation, confusion, and disorder to a place of measured predictability and security. He became a surgeon and certainly loved order. His life was a page out of Horatio Alger – second in his undergraduate class, first in his medical school class. As a scientist he believed, as Francis Bacon wrote, *"the true and lawful goal of the sciences is none other than this: that human life be endowed with new discoveries and powers."[31]* However, his adult life was hardly "green."

The word America is synonymous with "growth" the world over. To Medieval European populations already limited by dwindling wood energy supplies, the Lord's command of domination and subjugation was the natural order of the universe. The abundant natural resources of the New World were a seemingly endless call to expansion. The scientific advances in physics leading to the industrial revolution were simply God's gifts leading mankind out of primitive chaos to a more orderly world.

Growth is sewn into the fiber of America where "pursuit of Happiness" is translated to mean "pursuit of wealth or property." Based on God's mandate and the ringing bell of freedom, "Progress" is the amassing of greater and greater material abundance. The Twentieth Century is when the sciences and technology pushed America to its pinnacle of power and expansion. The American victories in two World Wars established moral justice but also brought the conviction that things just needed to be rearranged to bring them into the same order. The systematic demolition of the Hoosier Slide sand dune in my hometown was just a minute part of the transformation of the American landscape in the name of progress. The changes in my parents' lifetimes seem remarkable to me. When my parents got married my mother drove a still serviceable Ford Model "A." (Honest! I've seen the pictures.) When my father died near the turn of the Millennium, he owned two Mercedes.

The 1950s and 60s seemed a time of ultimate promise. The evidence of power could be seen, and smelled, and choked upon. I remember riding in one of the series of my father's Cadillacs, soaring toward Chicago along the expressway leading around the southern edge of Lake Michigan. America's industrial might was glorious in the leaping flames and billowing smoke from the mighty smokestacks of the Gary steel mills. It was truly breathless and we always rushed to close the car windows. But it all seemed good. More cars were good. More highways were good. More buildings were good. More people were good—or not really something we could do anything about. From 1930 to 1960 the world population increased from 2 billion to 3 billion people. But the necessary "growth" also provided jobs and the amassing of material abundance.

My father loved nature. He loved to get in an airplane, fly off on vacation and visit nature—usually to someplace warm, sunny and with a beach. Since the time of Teddy Roosevelt Americans have had a mission to protect nature—at least some nature—"over there" nature. It is the peculiarity of our national character that we have this deep conflict. We sing of "purple mountains majesty" and "fruited plains" and either plow them under or cover them over with subdivisions. We work hard at creating a mythology of nature where the image of the vastness and glory of our landscape is essential to our identity. We can't always see that nature behind the parking lots, bill boards and strip malls, but we know it's out there and it is ours. At some level my father understood the illusion. In 1957 he took my mother to Hawaii ... "before it all disappears."

For my grandfather, who repaired the firebrick linings of the great furnaces of the Pullman Standard factory, the source of the energy of industry was quite evident. It was heavy, black and dirty. The evidence stayed with him his remaining life in the form of emphysema and cardio-pulmonary heart disease (CPD). As a child I remember the oil tanker arriving to fill the underground tank that fed the oil-fired furnace in my father's new 1950s house. However, increasingly the source of our energy has become remote and abstract. Natural gas smells a bit. Flip a switch and the lights "magically" come on. The pain is in writing the check to pay the bill. My father invested in energy because he owned stock in oil wells—but I don't know if my father ever pumped his own gas to fill the tank of his car. Energy and the source of energy fuels were intellectual concepts for my father—and they continue to be just that for most of us.

In the 1950s and early 1960s—long before he was Governor of California or President, Ronald Reagan would appear regularly on the flickering black and white TV screens in American living rooms. He was a shill for the General Electric Company and the closing line in his commercials was always, "Progress is Our Most Important Product." Since GE was a manufacturer of appliances the message was pretty clear: "progress" meant more irons, refrigerators, washing machines. More stuff. And most of that stuff was activated by sticking a plug into a wall outlet—*cheap, abundant, readily available, magically easy, electricity*.

It was one of the national endeavors of the 1930s that electricity would be brought to every household through the government program called the Tennessee Valley Authority (TVA). In spite of his promotion of "progress," Reagan was fired from his TV job in 1962 for a critical analysis of the Tennessee Valley Authority. Reagan isn't known as a "green" president or even being environmentally friendly. However in this statement we see how our reliance on fossil fuels and human instinct to tame wild nature lead to absurd inefficiencies.

One such considered above criticism, sacred as motherhood, is TVA. This program started as a flood control project; the Tennessee Valley was periodically ravaged by destructive floods. The Army Engineers set out to solve this problem. They said that it was possible that once in 500 years there could be a total capacity flood that would inundate some 600,000 acres (2,400 km²). Well, the engineers fixed that. They made a permanent lake which inundated a million acres (4,000 km²). This solved the problem of floods, but the annual interest on the TVA debt is five times as great as the annual flood damage they sought to correct. Of course, you will point out that TVA gets electric power from the impounded waters, and this is true, but today 85 percent of TVA's electricity is generated in coal burning steam plants. Now perhaps you'll charge that I'm overlooking the navigable waterway that was created, providing cheap barge traffic, but the bulk of the freight barged on that waterway is coal being shipped to the TVA steam plants, and the cost of maintaining that channel each year would pay for shipping all of the coal by rail, and there would be money left over.[32]

In a world of seemingly endless abundance, the *image* of "progress" is sometimes more important than the reality of efficiency. That is not green.

The health of the American economy is measured in numbers. The radio, TV, and now the internet all report the Gross National Product, employment statistics, status of the Dow-Jones Industrial Average and other statistics related to the manufacturing segment of the economy. Most people would say that manufacturing is the essential element of our economic stability. However, the other often reported indicator of the economy is "housing starts." Economists realize that people buying new homes also tend to spend money on other consumer goods such as furniture, lawn and garden supplies, and home appliances. The overlooked truth is that the Construction

Industry is the largest industry in the United States and central to its operation is constant growth and transformation of our built environment.

Houses, apartments, factories, offices, schools, roads, and bridges are only some of the products of the construction industry. This industry's activities include the building of new structures, including site preparation, as well as additions and modifications to existing buildings and homes. The industry also includes maintenance, repair, and improvements on these structures. We can basically break employment in the construction industry into four major areas. The first is comprised of those who design. This group would include registered professionals such as architects, landscape architects, and (in some states) interior designers. Designers include all varieties of engineers: structural, mechanical and civil. Then there are all of those who work in design firms in technical and management support activities—drafting, computer aided design, project management, specification writing and more.

The second area of employment is made up of those who construct, including home builders, general contractors and all who work in these fields. The jobs involving physical labor are pretty obvious, but those less visible include estimating, scheduling and project management. This area of employment includes material supply and extends to steel, brick and lumber. The big home improvement box stores fall in this category and so do the local hardware stores. Finally, we must also fabricate the materials for the entire industry, which brings us back to manufacturing. Think of all of the components of the built environment, their development and manufacture, with most of the processes still taking place in the United States.

The third area of construction employment is finance. This area of employment includes bankers, lawyers, real estate agents, mortgage brokers and developers. Developers are in the business of financing or soliciting investors in new projects that will generate profit. The last area of employment involved in the construction industry is government, from the city to the federal level, which creates regulation and the enforcement of regulation. Employment includes building departments, planning departments, code and ordinance review, city engineers and surveyors, and building inspectors.

If the largest industry in the U.S is construction, then the health of the American economy depends on our continuing to build—a lot. When we were a young couple, my wife and I purchased some apartment buildings in a rundown beachfront area along the shores of Lake Michigan. These old buildings were originally built in the 1920s and had been divided up into small vacation apartments for the growing and vacationing families of the 1950s and 1960s. Absentee owners, lack of maintenance and the natural deterioration of building materials meant that by the early 1980s the entire neighborhood was pretty shoddy and ripe for investment. From the mid-1980s through the mid-1990s we rented the small apartments to doctors, nurses, lawyers, teachers, businessmen and businesswomen. The apartments were small but the beachfront location was desirable. Almost all of these tenants left when it became possible for them to purchase their own homes.

By 2002 our tenants were transient, unemployed, and on disability, and many had the attendant social problems of alcohol, drugs and family dysfunction. One young man died of a heroin overdose. How did this happen? During the 1990s interest rates were lowered and working people were able to buy homes. This meant that more homes had to be built, growing the American economy. The 1990s was a merry–go-round of financing and re-financing of property as the interest rates were successively lowered. We, too "cashed-in" on the equity in our homes by refinancing to renovate our buildings, send our kids to college and take a vacation or two. We certainly did our part to keep the construction economy going.

The developing problem was that the housing market was getting saturated. There was a point in the mid-1990s when most of the mortgages being approved were for peoples' *second* homes! The solution? Lending institutions lowered the requirements necessary to get a loan. Sub-prime mortgages were the fuel that kept the engine of the American Economy chugging along. Sub-prime mortgages meant that we as a country could continue to build houses and keep people employed in all of the interrelated jobs.

The urban history of the city on the shores of Lake Michigan, where my grandfather settled, is a record of the changes in consumerism that occurred in the second half of the 20th century. During the Christmas holidays it is inevitable that Frank Capra's, "It's a Wonderful Life" is shown on TV. I seem to always find time to curl up with some holiday goodies, for the hour or two to watch, and I always end with a good cry. I sometimes wonder if the tears are for the joy and relief of the rescue of George by his grateful neighbors, or a mourning for a world and town that has ceased to exist.

I realize that even in 1946 when the film was made, the world of George Bailey that Capra created, was one that was wished for more than one that actually existed. Nonetheless, whenever I see George running down the main street of Bedford Falls I think of the hometown of my childhood. One might say it was a "picture postcard" downtown; and indeed, I have bought several main street image postcards of my hometown on eBay. My favorite postcard depicts a summer parade with a classic high-hatted drum major marching in front of the ten-story downtown hotel.

The eleven-block business district had the major national stores, such as Sears, Kresge's, and Penney's, but most of the stores were locally owned businesses. There were two movie theaters and a popcorn wagon on the corner during the summer. The drug store had a soda fountain. People lived on adjacent streets and could walk to do their shopping. It was a downtown similar to cities all over the USA. And it was very similar to Bedford Falls. So what happened? In the early 1960s the theory of urban planning was "urban renewal." Some jokingly called it "urban removal." In effect, it was a man-made effort to replicate the economic benefits that some communities get from the devastation caused by natural disasters. So the bulldozers wiped out eight city blocks of the downtown, removing the oldest buildings in the city and displacing the residents. Unfortunately there were no concrete plans for what would be built on that land, some of which is still vacant 45 years later.

In 1967 the big shopping mall opened near the highway on the southern edge of the city. The collapse of the remaining urban core was almost immediate, with the national stores moving to the new location. In the 1970s the Interstate at the south of the city was completed. As an architect I believe that the built environment is a physical manifestation of the values of a culture in a particular time and place. In the 1980s and 90s the development in the open land between the city limits and the Interstate exit was a rubber stamp of the development found in every larger community: Wal-Mart, K-Mart, the national restaurant chains, and the large home improvement super stores. If you couldn't see the cooling tower of the lakefront electrical generating plant in the distance, you wouldn't know where you were. The rural corn fields, vineyards, and apple orchards that surrounded the urban center of the city have become a patchwork of subdivisions.

The factory where my grandfather helped manufacture railroad cars also closed down in the mid 1960s. In the following years the companies that manufactured boilers, plumbing parts, adhesive tape, and even men's pants, closed or moved their operations—sometimes to foreign countries. The local economy reflected the national trend toward service-based industries. The railroad car factory land, and all its building stock dating to the 19th century, was sold at auction. A year later a "mysterious" fire destroyed the complex. Soon after, that land was developed. It became a shining beacon of American consumerism: an outlet mall.

My mother's ancestors were immigrants. She came from Massachusetts and was a descendant of William Bradford, the Governor of the Plymouth colony established in 1620. My father was an immigrant, too—except he arrived in the US in 1927. Bradford and my father did have a common experience. The natives of Massachusetts weren't too happy about Bradford's arrival and neither were the citizens who confronted my father when he arrived at the age of 16 speaking no English. It seems to be a part of the American experience that the most recent arrivals are denigrated by the ones who came before them. It was an experience that affected my father his entire life. His striving for success was, in a large measure, a battle against those who discriminated against him in his youth.

But the American imperative for growth has required a constant expansion of the population—legal or illegal. Although the exact number is unknown, between 12 and 20 million illegal immigrants live in the United States. They are essential to an economy based on growth. They may be illegal, but they are still consumers. It seems obvious that in the loud and angry discussion regarding immigration, the real culprit may prove to be the American need for constant growth, along with the need for unskilled, low-wage labor.

My grandfather didn't have any problem understanding the direct link between the work of his hands, and the product that rolled out on the rail lines of the factory. His sweat, his scraped knuckles and the soot which besmirched his lungs helped build those railroad cars. During the 20th century and into the new millennium, for many people, there has been a disconnect in conscious understanding of the relationship of resources, work and consumables (stuff). A trip to Wal-Mart is an amazing event. Endless aisles of commodities magically appear, without any sense of the work it takes to produce them. In our global economy the work may truly have taken place on the other side of the planet, but that production work is faceless. The item that we want to buy becomes an object of desire; but the manner of its manufacture has no meaning.

Our post-Industrial Age consumables system separates man from the source of goods. Work becomes abstract, except personal work which even in manufacturing is often separated from the final product. Service industry work is even more isolated since there is no physical product. Today the largest employer in my home town community is the riverboat gambling casino, an operation that takes in a lot of cash without generating any real product.

Without a connection to the production of consumables, there is an even further distance to the understanding of the raw resources that are necessary for production. In my grandfather's Slovakian village there was an inherent understanding that sun, water, and some pig poop was necessary to grow the cabbage for sauerkraut. My father's effort to escape his ridiculed roots, like many immigrants of his generation, meant abandoning his culture. We lived a suburban life.

We did not have a garden. We had grass. My father grew up weeding cabbages. I grew up mowing a lawn. A green, verdant, expanse of grass was a symbol of financial status. It was a growing, living, representation of acquired abundance. My father was obsessed with the lawn, the sprinkler, the fertilizer. It was an ongoing struggle with a non-compliant nature that refused to bend to his will. We lived on the shores of Lake Michigan. We had plenty of sand but not much top soil. At one point in my childhood the entire lawn was ripped out and replaced with fresh sod. There was no concern that the grass was without any productive value whatsoever, (beyond producing a bit of oxygen). Man must dominate!

In 1972 *The Limits to Growth* was published[33], modeling the consequences of a rapidly growing world population and finite resource supplies. The controversial conclusions predicted an eventual inability of resources to meet the demand of an exponentially growing population.

The apparent necessity of growth is so deeply entrenched in our world view that most people can't even imagine a way of questioning it. My father certainly didn't question it. Our former Vice-President Cheney, a man with a stake in maintaining a petroleum based worldview, stated it like this: "Here we aim to continue a path of uninterrupted progress in many fields...New technologies are proving that we can save energy without sacrificing our standard of living. And we're going to encourage it in every way possible."[34] And I assume that includes growing grass (with petroleum-based fertilizer, herbicides, and pesticides).

There is a growing conviction that the technology of our fathers may itself be the problem. We cannot endure exponential growth. Technology that continues to deplete the earth and diminish the human spirit cannot solve the problems that our father's technology has created. We must create new technological solutions that preserve, protect, and nurture us and all that we touch. A technology appropriate for the work it must do – nothing more and nothing less. A technology that produces necessities which can be usefully returned to the resource stream with minimum entropy. A technology that supports our lives but doesn't rule our lives.

Our grandfathers and fathers have left to us the world they built with their sweat—the one they fought for with their blood. It is the world they literally dug from deep in the ground to hand to us. As children we must grow up. In spite of their love, our parents have handed us a dysfunctional world. The essence of maturity and healing is forgiveness. The hardest part of entering the Green Age may be forgiving our fathers (and mothers) for screwing up the earth so badly.

Part Four:
Interconnections

In Part Four we explain the transition that must happen in our minds in order to take our worldview from the now antiquated Industrial Age and bring it into the Green Age. In order to do this we examine the mechanical version of material connection that goes with industrial age values and beliefs. We metaphorically "take our brains by the hand" and walk them into a new way of thinking. We take this esoteric "walk" by looking at discoveries that seemed like anomalies at the time they were made.

We start with the Industrial Age view in which the universe is compared to a mechanical clockwork. Then we move through discoveries in which numbers are found to be organizing principles in materiality and give us a first glimmer of interconnectivity—these are the Greek letter phi, the Fibonacci numbers, the Golden Section, and the Golden Spiral. We continue our "walk" through the ways in which human beings have been found to be interconnected, and end up with the twentieth century discovery of the actual connectivity of the material world in its entirety. This transition into seeing the material world as it actually is with its profound interconnectivity is critical.

Chapter 5:
The First Glimmers of the Universe as an Interconnected System

In 1605 the astronomer Johannes Kepler thought he understood the secret of the Universe. In a letter he wrote, "My aim is this, to show that the celestial machine is to be likened not to a divine living thing but rather to a clockwork (Horologium)…" It's an idea that has stuck. The underlying principle of modern science is that if we just take the world apart and examine the pieces like the gears of some old alarm clock, the secrets of the universe will be revealed. Even the great spiritual master of our age, the Dali Lama, confesses a boyhood fascination with clocks – taking them apart to see how they worked at every chance he could get. While studying at the feet of the great Buddhist teachers he also fixed their broken watches.

The problem with this approach is that it separates the examiner from the examined. The universe is rendered into a tabletop with a bunch of scattered gears—forgetting that we are one of them. It is the malaise of our age, generating disorder and dysfunction.

Matt's Story

A misanthropic classmate once confided his philosophical anguish with this dualistic dilemma while we were eating together in the college dining hall. "I keep trying to take apart the universe and look at the parts getting to smaller and smaller pieces. When I finally get down to the last atom, I cut it open. Inside is a little note that says, "Despair." At that point the student across the table, clearly not enjoying the cosmic conversation, threw down his fork and said, "Please! I'm eating my lunch!" Bummer, man.

"Many writers and commentators are suggesting that the current worldview or paradigm of Western civilization is reaching the end of its useful life. It is suggested that there is a fundamental shift occurring in our understanding of the universe and our place in it, that new patterns of thought and belief are emerging that will transform our experience, our thinking and our action."[35] The fundamentals for these changes were laid out by Henryk Skolimowski in a pioneering 10 minute address delivered in London, England at the Architectural Association in 1974.

While participating in a discussion about the problems of alternative technology, Skolimowski radically posited that the precepts that create technology are themselves the problem. He rejects "the damaging assumption that the world is a clock-like mechanism within which we are little cogs and wheels. It has led us to reduce everything, including human life, to the status of components of this great machine. The consequences have been disastrous."[36]

Skolimowski argued that what is needed is a fundamentally different way of thinking. "Only when we find a new metaphor and invent a new conception of the world shall we be able to stand up to the senseless, destructive forces that have swept over our lives."[37] While most of the scientific world seems to look at little disconnected pieces, the science of ecology concentrates on interconnections. Ecological study focuses on the patterns and relationships of living systems in relation to their environment. The extension of ecological concepts encourages a holistic approach to the human relationship to nature, connecting communities and systems. Basically, it's all interconnected.

Like most secrets, the secret to the universe may be simple if we can just open our eyes to see. Certainly, one of those secrets is found in a number. 1.6180339887499 is represented by the Greek letter phi (φ). It is one of those mysterious natural numbers that seem to arise out of the basic structure of our cosmos. Phi appears clearly and regularly in the realm of things great and small that grow and unfold in steps, and that includes living things. One of those living things seems to be rabbits.

Rabbits, rabbits, rabbits. In the early 11th century, the Italian born Leonardo Fibonacci described in his book Liber Abaci tells how to optimize the breeding of rabbits. Fibonacci's plan was that each rabbit pair produces another pair every month, taking one month first to mature, and continuing to increase...well, like rabbits. Each number in the sequence is the sum of the previous two. 0, 1, 1, 2, 3, 5, 8, 13, 21, 34, 55, 89, 144, ... to infinity. In short order you have a lot of rabbits.

It turns out that Fibonacci was one of the greatest mathematicians of the Middle Ages. Fibonacci grew up in North Africa where he observed the mathematical systems of the Mediterranean merchants. In his book *Liber Abaci* he explained to the Latin world of Europe the use of the Hindu Arabic numeral system with its nine digits, symbol for zero and the decimal. He also reported one of the great patterns of the universe in his rabbit breeding scheme, which has been named the Fibonacci series.

One place we find the Fibonacci series is in growing plants. The process of the growing plant follows the Fibonacci numbers, from the first shoot, to the two shoots, three shoots, and five shoots, and eight shoots, and on and on. Flower petals emerge as Fibonacci numbers.

The branching rates in trees occur in the Fibonacci pattern, where the first level has one "branching" (the trunk), the second has two branches, then 3, 5, 8, 13 and so on.

Cut open a fruit and inside you find divisions based on Fibonacci numbers. A banana has three segments, an apple five. [38]

If you then take the ratio of any two sequential numbers in the Fibonacci series, you'll find that it falls into an increasingly narrow range:

$1/1 =$ 1
$2/1 =$ 2
$3/2 =$ 1.5
$5/3 =$ 1.6666...
$8/5 =$ 1.6
$13/8 =$ 1.625
$21/13 =$ 1.61538...
$34/21 =$ 1.61904...

and so on, with each addition coming ever closer to multiplying by some as-yet-undetermined number.

The number that this ratio is oscillating around is **phi** (1.6180339887499...), and is the underlying pattern and rhythm of the universe, called the Golden Section. Phi ratios were the basis of the proportional system developed by the classical Greeks, and can be found in all Greek and Roman temples. It provided a means of creating a satisfying order, in what otherwise seemed to be a chaotic world ruled by capricious gods. It was rediscovered during the Renaissance, in a book written by a first century Roman architect named Vitruvius. As an underlying cosmic theme its importance was recognized by the movers and shakers of the Renaissance. In 1509 Luca Paccioli wrote a book on the Golden Section which he called the "divine proportion."

The Golden Section is a ratio or proportion defined by the number Phi. It can be derived with a number of geometric constructions, each of which divides a line segment at the unique point where:

the ratio of the whole line (A) to the large segment (B)

is the same as

the ratio of the large segment (B) to the small segment (C).

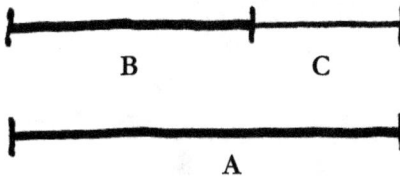

In other words, A is to B as B is to C.

This occurs only where A is 1.618... times B
and B is 1.618... times C.

Alternatively, C is 0.618... of B and B is 0.618... of A.

Leonardo da Vinci, who spent a lot of time looking into the secrets of the universe, did extensive study of proportion and the measurements of the human body, only to find continuous repetition of the Golden Section. Based on his study of the writings of Vitruvius, he produced one of the most recognizable drawings of the Renaissance. There in Leonardo's ink scratches, is proportional perfection. The humanist ideal is shown as man created in the image of God, sprawled spread eagle across a circle and a square.

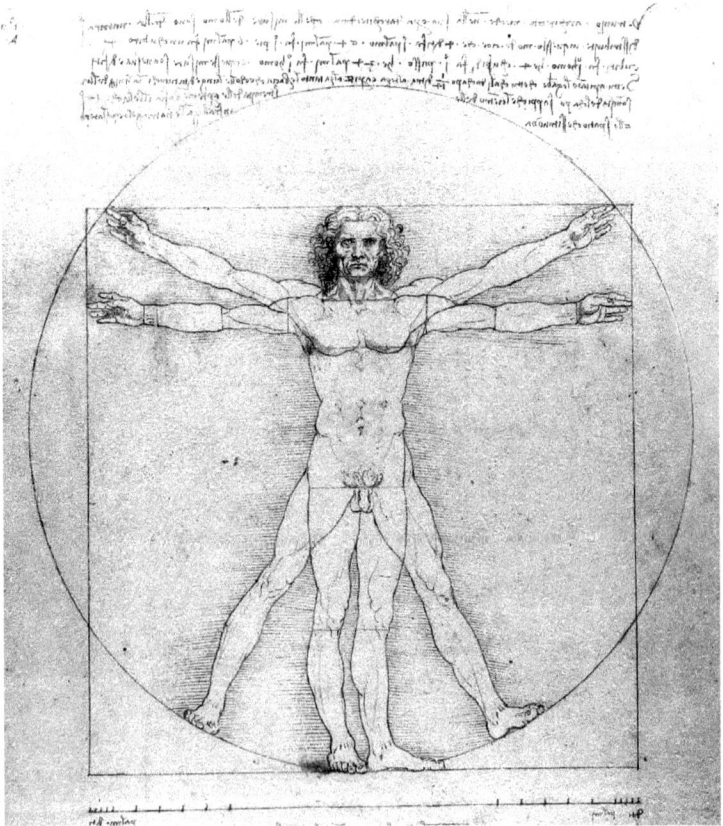

As Leonardo discovered, The Golden Section is found in the human body in an extraordinary series of relationships.[39] Using one of Leonardo's anatomical drawings the proportional relationships can by charted from full body height to fingertips.

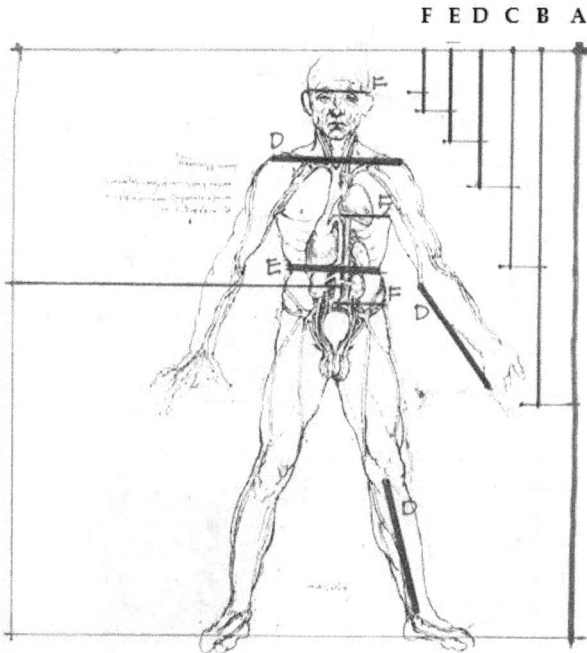

Line **A** is the body's height.

Line **B**, a Golden Section of Line A, defines the distance from the head to the fingertips.

Line **C**, a Golden Section of Line B defines the distance from the head to the navel.

Line **D**, a Golden Section of Line C, defines the width of the shoulders, the length of the forearm and the shin bone.

Line **E**, a Golden Section of Line D, defines the distance from the head to the base of the skull and the width of the abdomen.

Line **F**, a Golden Section of Line E, defines the width of the head, and ½ width of the chest and hips.

Appreciation of the proportional harmony that is contained in the form and structure of the human body seems to be the essence of art and design esthetics. Geometrically, the Golden Section is expressed as perfectly proportioned squares and rectangles. In ideal architecture the proportions extend to volumetric space.

A Golden Section can be simply constructed by bisecting a 1 foot X 1 foot square then constructing an arc with the center as the base of the Centerline and a Radius taken from the diagonal corner. The resulting extension of the base line is Phi 1.618. The continued expansion of this operation creates a figure known as the Golden Spiral.

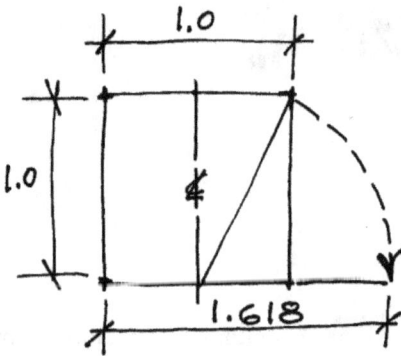

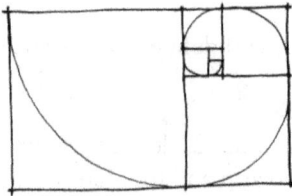

This is the geometric construction of a form very close to the logarithmic spiral. The spiral is a form that occurs in nature in many forms and at many scales. On the beach the shell under your feet curls inward corkscrewing in tighter and tighter turns seemingly to infinity — the Golden Spiral. We see it in the world around us every day—but we don't often recognize it. In your garden you may see seeds of a yellow sunflower spiraling outwards. There it is in the twisting spurt of a plant tendril. There again in the turning hardness of a ram's horn.

Satellites have allowed us to take global self-portraits of both benign and destructive forces. On September 14, 2003, Hurricane Isabel, spinning turbulence of vaporous violence, passed 400 miles north of Puerto Rico. NASA's Aqua satellite snapped a photograph.[40] If beauty can be found in the dynamic force of nature, it is there in Isabel's glorious Golden Spiral.

After seven years of design and construction one of the world's largest and most powerful telescopes opened its shutters in the spring of 2001. It turned its 8.1 metre-wide mirror toward the skies to capture its first light on the summit of a dormant volcano on Hawaii's Big Island. The $5 million Gemini North Telescope, was designed to take advantage of pristine, clear skies over 4,200 metres (14,000 ft) high at the Observatories at Mauna Kea. Astronomers chose for the instrument's first light image the large galaxy in Pisces called NGC 628 (or Messier 74).[41] In many ways this is the smaller twin brother of our Milky Way at about 100 billion stars. This galaxy is more than 30 million light years away from us and helps to give some perspective as to what our own galaxy might look like if beings from another planet had a telescope focused toward Earth, looking back at us. So what do we see in this astounding image captured by Gemini North? Star clusters, gas clouds and dust lanes similar to what we can see in our own Milky Way with a small telescope or even the naked eye. But there is more. In the glitter and sparkling swirl of the cosmos, is a form—so beautiful that the astronomers named this galaxy, "The Perfect Spiral".

Chapter 6:
Glimmers of Interconnectedness
in Human Beings

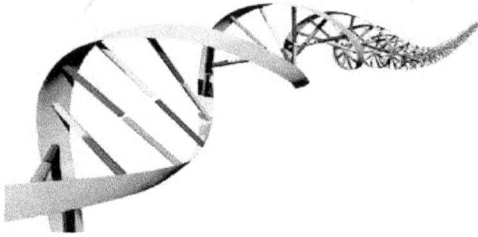

From the infinite reaches of the universe to the view through an electron microscope, we are connected in unexpected ways. Just four chemicals—adenine, cytosine, thymine and guanine—arranged in two pairs, are the fundament of all the life on earth in its enormous variety. From the smallest bacteria to the largest mammal it is all structured from those two pairs of chemicals, arranged in enormously long sequences spinning into what we know as a double helix of DNA (deoxyribonucleic acid).

Genes are segments of each strand, consisting of several hundred thousand to over a million base pairs of nucleotides (the two basic pairs of chemicals). DNA is small—very small. It measures 34 angstroms long by 21 angstroms wide for each full cycle of its double helix spiral. 34 and 21, of course, are numbers in the Fibonacci series and their ratio, 1.6190476, closely approximates Phi, 1.6180339. Like its swirling galactic counterpart it is based on the Golden Section.

If stretched out, a DNA strand is 1.8 metres long and contains some 30,000 genes and is present in every one of the more than 75 trillion cells in the human body. Those 30,000 genes are responsible for the production of the 250,000 proteins which our bodies rely upon to maintain their life and health. All of this is stuffed into a cell nucleus, which is a mere one-hundredth of a millimeter in diameter.

The bacteria from which life on Earth has originated contained a set of genes that has created common genes between species. Of the 30,000 genes that provide the genetic makeup of human beings, only 300 of them are not shared with a mouse. A dog is nearly identical to human genetic sequences, with just a 15% difference. A fruit fly shares 15,000 of our 30,000 genes, and the earthworm shares 20,000 of our genes.

Anyone who watches the forensics-based police and crime shows on television knows that each person can be identified uniquely through DNA traces. However, we also carry common DNA with every other human on earth. By tracking DNA it has been determined that there was a woman whose mitochondrial DNA (with mutations) exists in **all** the humans now living on Earth. We all have a common mama. She is called Mitochondrial Eve, not in any way to be confused with characters found in biblical Genesis. While each of us necessarily has two parents, we get our mitochondria and mitochondrial DNA from the ovum (and hence from our mothers). Our mothers got their mitochondrial DNA from their mothers and so on. Estimates differ on when this mother lived because of undetermined rates of DNA mutation but it could be as few as 200,000 years ago!

In actuality our genetic diversity is fairly amazing. Mitochondrial Eve is the common matrilineal ancestor tracked through DNA. However, she is not the most recent common ancestor of all humans. That person could have lived as recently as 3,000 years ago. As we track our ancestors backward through time, each of them double with each generation. Two parents from four grandparents, from 16 great grandparents, 32 great, great grandparents, etc. The progression is exponential and it isn't too many years in the past and you find theoretically more ancestors than were alive at that point in history. Of course the answer is that there was a lot of commingling between folks who were fairly closely related. That can certainly be seen in the marriages of the Pilgrims who frequently married first and second cousins, due to the rather low number of available marital prospects.

It doesn't take much genealogical investigation to discover that through a common ancestor you may be related to any number of famous or infamous people living today. It is a fun pastime to figure out who is closely related to whom. Barack Obama, George W. Bush, and Queen Elizabeth II are all cousins if you go back about 12 generations when they share a common ancestor.[42] As far as we know no one has asked them how they feel about that. But the reality is that between one-hundred and two-hundred generations back, a single person will appear in every living person's family tree.[43] We are all related. How do *you* feel about that?

You and Queen Elizabeth II may share some mitochondrial DNA back a hundred thousand years. You could also find a more recent common ancestor if the records existed back several millennia. Socially you and the Queen may be a lot closer. How about six handshakes away? In a world of over 6.6 billion people it seems difficult to believe but the theory of six degrees of separation seems to be nearly accurate.

Kevin Bacon may be as famous for the game "Six Degrees of Kevin Bacon" as he is for his dancing in the movie "Footloose." In 1994 students at Pennsylvania's Albright College invented the game, in which the challenge was to connect every film actor to Bacon in six cast lists or fewer. The idea came from the John Guare 1990 play, *Six Degrees of Separation*, which was turned into a film starring Will Smith, Stockard Channing, Donald Sutherland and Ian McKellen.

A 'degree of separation' is a measure of social distance between people. You are one degree away from everyone you know, two degrees away from everyone they know, and so on. In the play one of the characters says: "I read somewhere that everybody on this planet is separated by only six other people: six degrees of separation between us and everyone else on this planet. The President of the United States, a gondolier in Venice, just fill in the names. I find it, A, extremely comforting that we're so close and B, like Chinese water torture that we're so close. Because you have to find the right six people to make the right connection. It's not just big names. It's anyone.... I am bound to everyone on this planet by a trail of six people."[44]

It turns out the social distance is 6.6 degrees. Researchers at Microsoft studied records of 30 billion electronic conversations among 180 million people in various countries during June 2006. Eric Horvitz, one of the researches said, "To me it was pretty shocking. What we're seeing suggests there may be a social connectivity constant for humanity. People have had the suspicion that we are really close. But we are showing on a very large scale that this idea goes beyond folklore."[45] It is an extraordinary realization that one might contact the Queen, the Pope, or even Kevin Bacon, if one put the power of the 6.6 degree social network to work. How much closer have we grown since 2006 with the global access to cell phone communication and expansion of social networking through Facebook, LinkedIn, and Twitter?

What happens if we track the linkage of 6 handshakes through history. Let's use your own family history as an example. If you knew your grandfather and your grandfather knew his grandfather and so on, how far back in time would you reach with six connections. Assume an average generational distance of 60 years between child and grandparent. A child born in 2000 would be only 3 handshakes away from an ancestor who fought in the Civil War and four handshakes from the family Revolutionary War hero. He is six handshakes away from his ancestor living in the Plymouth Colony in 1640. Looking forward the child born in 2000 is only six kisses away from descendants living in 2360.

The understanding of this minimal social distance is the essence of the fundamental ethical statement found in almost all world religions. You probably know it as the Golden Rule. It is a call to self-monitoring behavior that provides to others the benefits of peace and comfort that one seeks for oneself. The "Declaration Toward a Global Ethic" from the Parliament of the World's Religions meeting in 1993 recognized the Golden Rule as the common principle and a unifying force for many religions.[46] The initial Declaration was signed by 143 leaders from different faith traditions and spiritual communities. This basic ethical principle is restated in many forms with the same basic message.

Here are a few examples:

Ancient Egypt: Do for one who may do for you, that you may cause him thus to do.[47]

Classical Greece: Do not do unto others what angers you if done to you by others.[48]

Imperial Rome: Treat your inferiors as you would be treated by your superiors.[49]

Judaism: You shall not take vengeance or bear a grudge against your kinsfolk. Love your neighbor as yourself: I am the LORD.[50]

Hinduism: This is the sum of duty: do not do to others what would cause pain if done to you.[51]

Islam: None of you [truly] believes until he wishes for his brother what he wishes for himself.[52]

Christianity: Love your neighbor as yourself[53]

Beyond the mere ordering of social interaction is the statement which can lead us to an ethical structure for the Green Age, extracted as the essential basis for all interactions with the physical world. The recognition must be that we humans and all living things are the weft and warp of the same fabric. From the swirling planets to the twisting DNA there is an interconnection that makes us inseparable from each other and even inseparable from all existence.

> Love the universe as yourself.
> Love the Earth as yourself.
> Love your neighbor as yourself.
> It's the same thing.

Few people have ever been in the position to look out at our home planet through the window of a human-constructed orbiting space craft. It must be somewhat of a shock to see our planet as a whole entity rather than the bits and pieces that are the usual subject of scientific investigation. The sun pours new energy onto what is otherwise a totally closed system of finite resources in circular energy flow...including humans. From

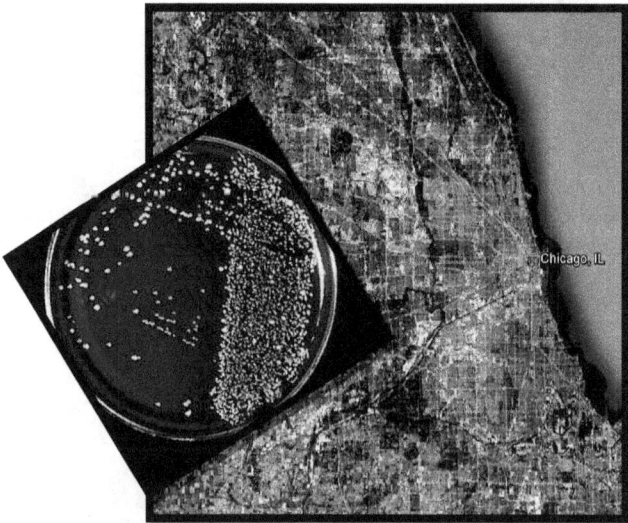

outer space expanding human influence on the planet surface looks like bacteria multiplying in a laboratory Petri dish—also a closed system with boundary limits. A common laboratory experiment shows that the bacteria expands to the limits of the environment and then collapses. We as humans risk the same fate if we can't balance growth with resource use

The study of ecology is essentially the study of community interactions within certain earth environments. It is in reality the study of energy flow in those environments. As we look at the global ecosystem we see that humans are integral conduits of energy which flows from the sun to the earth, through us individually and collectively, then back to the earth and into the atmosphere.

We are thermodynamic entities. As early as 1874, German scientist Ernst von Brucke proposed that all living organisms are energy-systems governed by the principle of the conservation of energy. Brucke was also, coincidentally, the supervisor at the University of Vienna for first-year medical student Sigmund Freud, who adopted this new paradigm. Freud argued that both the first law of thermodynamics and the second law of thermodynamics apply to mental processes, and posited the existence of a mental energy set to function according to these laws.

Freud's colleague Carl Jung could not have known that we are connected by the Fibonacci structure of our DNA to the form of the galaxies, carrying the DNA of a woman who lived long before recorded history. Nor could he have known that we are only a few introductions away from every other living human. Nonetheless he proposed the idea of Collective Unconscious in his development of analytical psychology. It is a part of the unconscious mind, shared by a society, a people, or all humanity, that is the product of ancestral experience and contains such concepts as science, religion, and morality.

While Freud did not distinguish between an "individual psychology" and a "collective psychology," Jung distinguished the collective unconscious from the personal subconscious, particular to each human being. The collective unconscious is also known as "a reservoir of the experiences of our species."[54]

Chapter 7:
Material Interconnectivity

The interconnectivity that is shown on the mathematical level by the Golden Spiral, on the physical, human level by our common ancestor, and on the level of consciousness by Jung and our collective unconscious, can also be found at the smallest level of material life. Buckminster Fuller is a profound thinker of the twentieth century. In the following quote he reveals one of the basic insights that physics has discovered about the way that matter itself is structured. It turns out that **all of life** at the level of subatomic particles **is a continuous whole**.

> "In short, physics has discovered
> that there are no solids,
> no continuous surfaces,
> no straight lines;
> only waves,
> no things
> only energy event complexes,
> only behaviors,
> only verbs,
> only relationships.[55]"

When we look at the smallest particles of matter, what we observe is that there is no actual separation in materiality at all. Subatomic particles are so completely interconnected, interrelated, and interdependent, that they are not even able to be understood as isolated particles, but can only be understood within the context of their related phenomena as integral parts of a whole. What physics helps us to understand is that everything that exists is a field of unbroken wholeness. This means that the classical idea of looking at and analyzing the world as if it were made up of individual separate parts that exist independently of one another isn't helpful. In fact, quantum physics reverses the ideas about the world that we have held. We have always looked at the parts that appear to be individually functioning as the fundamental reality, and we've regarded the systems that these parts create as they work together as simply contingent arrangements of the parts. Instead, it is the "inseparable quantum interconnectedness of the whole universe" that is fundamentally real, and the parts that appear to be independent that are the contingent forms within the whole.[56]

The consequences of this interconnectedness on our efforts to conduct any scientific investigation of any particular event is that the particles constituting the material world can **only** be understood as an undivided whole, and that includes the particles of which "human beings, their laboratories, [and] observing instruments" are made.[57] Stated somewhat differently, thinking about any particle of matter as existing independently makes no sense at all. And we are made, as is the entire natural, biological, material world, of these particles that must be viewed through the lens of quantum interconnectedness in order to be coherently understood—to make sense.

As Fuller has stated in the quote that opens this discussion, physics has discovered that there are no solid things. Not only is there nothing that is actually solid—everything is an "energy event complex" made up of waves, behaviors, verbs, and relationships. What does that mean? It means that when we look at life in its smallest particles, we see molecules, atoms, electrons, protons, neutrons, neutrinos, quarks, and so on, moving around and interacting with each other. They do not stop at the periphery of the epidermis on one person and begin again at the outer layer of skin of the person standing next to them. They do not stop at the landfill and begin again at the water table that lies beneath. They are amassed together more tightly within the confines of the person's skin or the water's surface, but they don't stop at the visible edges.

These minute, active, and ever-changing particles that are the stuff of our physical, material earth continue along indefinitely, interacting and inter-relating with all the other minute and active particles that make up the earth and the universe. In fact, if our vision were ultra-microscopic rather than 20-20, it would be hard to discern where one thing ends and anything else begins.

Understanding the natural environment through the lens of this existing interconnectedness (the structure of matter), and the laws of thermodynamics (the way units of matter work together), and its implied meaning—that everything is an energy event complex, we can now see that every existing unit of matter in nature moves/grows/becomes/changes, within this inter-connected structure and following these laws. These are the embedded conditions of life on earth that contributes to nature's biological flourishing.

Think about how the atoms, molecules, and cells of the human and animal bodies of the world exhibit these embedded conditions by interacting and interrelating with each other quite automatically—all of them working together toward the common outcome of creating the living bodies that are you and me. Each minute, living part does its own individual job, to the best of its ability. We don't have to give directions or orders! No need to tell our hearts to beat or our lungs to go about the business of distributing the oxygen that we inhale. The entire work that goes on in the body is a creation of synchronous and intuitively interactive movement—a million individual elements, all striving toward flourishing!

We grew up thinking that our intelligence is located in our heads, and the brain has been regarded as the physical part of us that is in charge of the entire system. But biologists now tell us that conceiving of ourselves in this way is completely inaccurate. Our cells are not just robotically living out a preprogrammed genetic code given to them by our DNA. In fact, the membranes of our cells have "receptor proteins" and "effector proteins" that respond to environmental signals with intelligence. In multicellular organisms like us, cells have responded to their environment to work efficiently and intelligently together. So for example, whereas a single cell "breathes" with its mitochondria, in our bodies billions of cells have specialized as a mitochondrial function and work together to form the lungs. And in the same way that a single cell moves through the interaction of two proteins called actin and myosin, the muscles in our bodies that enable us to move are created by communities of cells, which have enormous quantities of these proteins, working together collaboratively to fulfill the task of mobility.[58]

Think about the natural process of photosynthesis, and how the elementary units of nature all work together to create an organic movement that fosters a prospering, a flourishing of other organic, biological units of nature. When trees use carbon dioxide from our planet's air and produce oxygen, it creates a process that allows us human beings to live and thrive. But we must have plenty of trees in order for that to happen because we are biophilic—oxygen-breathing organic beings—and without the tiny cells in the leaves of the trees constantly turning sunlight and carbon dioxide into oxygen through the biological, organic, process of photosynthesis, we would have nothing to inhale that would actually be able to sustain our lives.

In 1966, Stewart Brand, the founder of the *Whole Earth Catalog*, initiated a public campaign to have NASA release the then-rumored satellite image of the sphere of Earth, as seen from space. He thought the image of our planet might be a powerful symbol that would evoke adaptive strategies from people. The image of our Earth[59] (next page) was a revelation! When it was finally published it was the first time that we human beings had seen ourselves from outside the Earth's atmosphere. Our planet is a beautiful, swirly, blue marble. We became aware that it is self-contained and fragile.

Now think about how the planets, stars and suns all move together in this same synchronous way. Think about the earth, and about all of the interactive processes that take place in order for life to continue along, grow and develop here in this lush "garden of Eden" that we call home. Think about the simple action of our breathing and all that has to take place automatically, both inside of the biological unit that we think of as ourselves and outside of that biological unit, in order for our bodies to inhale and exhale. It is essential that we keep the interconnectedness of the material world and its working systems in mind in order to maintain an environment that is supportive of and sustaining to human life and to the land community with whom we co-inhabit this earth, our home.[60]

Part Five:
The Green Age

In Part Five we examine the Green Age Worldview and begin by re-thinking the meaning of "progress." When we make progress, we feel we've moved in a positive direction toward something desirable. ***In the Green Age, we would feel we were making progress if the actions we take serve to ensure that the Earth is able to sustain itself and its inhabitants***—that is, what we do nourishes it so well that it is able to provide nourishment for current and future inhabitants. No decision would be made or action would be taken that didn't ultimately have this value at its core. In this section we discuss our personal journeys toward this goal.

Chapter 8:
Green Age Worldview

"Go forth and sustain the World:
the 21st (century) commandment."

Edgar D. Mitchell, Astronaut[61]

So what would a Green Age be? Let's review. Human beings living as hunter-gatherers engaged in a subsistence food strategy that was primary for approximately two million years. Then around twelve thousand years ago, horticultural practices of growing food began being implemented in different areas around the world, including the Middle East, Asia, Mesoamerica, and the Andes. And in a relatively short time (by comparison)— a few thousand years—the Agricultural Age burst into full bloom. It began in about 8,000 BCE and lasted until approximately 1800 CE[62]—just ten thousand years. Being able to cultivate and rely on our food sources gave us time to focus more extensively on other things, though it led to the institution of social classes and the state, and to systematic warfare.

We've now been living in the Industrial Age, with its accompanying mechanical focus for just three-hundred years. In that time we have seriously depleted and despoiled the planet. We have disrupted the ties of mutuality that bound us together in communities. We have defined self-development almost entirely in terms of the consumption of (ultimately unsustainable) material goods. And so it's time to change. We must enter the Green Age. And we must do it rapidly.

If we can in fact, successfully enter the Green Age, in a couple of thousand years humans might not even regard, the Industrial Age as an Age, but rather as a transitional time in our human story—one during which we moved from the Agricultural Age directly into the Green Age. Of course we didn't set out to "foul our nest" at the advent of the Industrial Age. We were simply caught up in the idea of what progress meant to us. It is time to change the meaning of progress as we move into the future of our human story.

Because values and beliefs are the underlying framework of our worldview, and because our worldview provides the basis of the automatic choices we make in our everyday lives, we must begin by imagining the values and beliefs that will assist in sustaining the Earth and its inhabitants. As we have seen, the importance of these values and beliefs cannot be understated. If we want to enter the Green Age, then we must ensure that we have adopted an appropriate set of beliefs and values.

Consider the following story. Imagine that you have an empty one-liter container and a pile of small rocks. If you put the rocks into the container in a tight fit such that no additional rocks can fit, is the container now full? No, because there are air spaces between the rocks. So imagine that you pour gravel into the container and shake it so that the gravel fills in the spaces. Now is the container full? No. There are still air spaces. So now you pour sand into the container, shaking it so that the sand fills in the spaces. Is the container now finally full? No. Imagine that you pour water into the container until it reaches the very top. Is the container now completely full, in that nothing more can be added to it without displacing existing contents? Yes, it is full.

What is the moral of this story? Most Americans would say something along the lines of "You can always squeeze in more stuff." That is, no matter how busy you are, you can always do more. However, a far more important moral—especially for our purposes here—is this: "Put the big stuff in first." If we had started with the sand and gravel, there would have been no room for the bigger rocks. What are the big rocks in our lives? They are our values. We must, first and foremost, be sure to spend our time and energy on the things most important to us. At the end of the day, if we don't have room for a few pebbles or grains of sand, it is of little consequence. But if we leave out substantial rocks, we will significantly impoverish our lives and make it nearly impossible to enter the Green Age.

But how do we imagine values and beliefs that will exist inside of an Age that we haven't yet entered? One way to begin is to examine those values and beliefs that we currently hold and interpret them through the lens of the new worldview to see what they look like. We'll begin by re-thinking the meaning of "progress." As we said earlier, when we make progress, we feel we've moved in a positive direction toward something desirable.

In the Green Age we would feel we were making progress if the actions we take serve to ensure that the Earth is able to sustain itself and its inhabitants—that is, what we do nourishes the earth so well that it is able to provide nourishment for current and future inhabitants. This would then be the central value. No decision would be made or action would be taken that didn't ultimately have this value at its core. And most importantly, in order to figure out whether or not an action would sustain the Earth, we would need to consider the action in its largest possible realm of connectivity, as a part of a whole system that is Earth itself. Arran Stibbe and Heather Luna call this approach *sustainability literacy*. As people develop these skills, they say, "they become empowered to read society critically, discovering insights into the unsustainable trajectory that society is on and the social structures that underpin this trajectory. But more than this, they become empowered to engage with those social structures and contribute to the re-writing of self and society along more sustainable lines." The primary value of *sustaining the Earth* would reorder how we think about everything else. As Sim van der Ryn and Stuart Cowan note, "It is time to stop designing in the image of the machine and start designing in a way that honors the complexity and diversity of life itself."[63] In this context, what would happen to the values that were prominent in the Industrial Age, like *locomotion, speed, precision, accuracy, distance, hyper-efficiency, predictability, calculability, control, short term, disposable, expediency, conquest, colonizing, expansion, survival of the fittest, and having no limits*? What would we do with them? Would they continue to be values, and simply be subjugated to the primary value of *sustaining the Earth*? Or would we toss them? And with what would we replace them? It is relatively easy to see what our values are in the Industrial Age, because they are writ large on the television screen in the form of commercials. For the Green Age, we'll have to use a different technique to illuminate our values. Let's imagine a future based on the value of *sustaining the Earth and its inhabitants.*

Pat's Story

I grew up on the East Side of Detroit. It was a lower middle class urban neighborhood of tiny lots and small brick houses. The families were mostly first- and second-generation Italians and Poles. A majority of the men worked in the auto industry. We moved in when I was three years old. One of my earliest memories was of the regular trips of the "sheeny man" down the alley on warm summer afternoons.

Years later I discovered that *sheeny* was an ethnic slur used against Jewish immigrants. But in my time the sheeny man was African American. To us kids he seemed like an old man, though he was probably in his 40s or 50s. Sometimes he had graying hair, though missing teeth most likely made him seem older. He was probably a recent immigrant from the Deep South who, due to persistent racism, couldn't get a job in the auto industry and had to survive on the margins of the economy.

In the late 1950s, the sheeny man arrived in a horse-drawn flatbed cart, with homemade stakes and odd strands of rope holding a precariously balanced stash of treasure scrounged from alleyways. While the massive horse shuffled slowly along, the sheeny man announced his presence in a rhythmic singsong that was unintelligible to us, except for the drawn-out word SHEEEEEEEE-NEE. It was hard to say which was more amazing—a horse or a Black man in our White ethnic urban neighborhood.

As soon as we heard his song, we kids made a beeline for the alley. We often scrounged for stuff to give him, just so he would stop and let us pat the horse and we could listen to the sheeny man's (to us) exotic accent. In later years (probably due to city regulations), the sheeny man switched to a beat-up old pickup truck, but he didn't ride as high or as openly and it was harder for him to make his song heard. And then as racial tensions heated up, it became too dangerous for a Black man to be in a White neighborhood in Detroit.

With the demise of the sheeny man, I took up patrolling the neighborhood alleys myself (minus the rhythmic song!). The sheeny man had taught me that almost nothing should be thrown out—everything could be reused by someone in some way. Moreover, my dad, a child of the Great Depression, was a creative handyman. He had a genius for building and fixing things that involved the creative reuse of materials, and I was his primary assistant. For instance, when we moved into the house, there was a large wheeled wooden cart that covered the two laundry tubs in the basement when they were not in use. My dad turned it on its end and, using scrounged wood and old cabinet doors left in the basement, turned it into a cabinet for our toys.

Five children in a tiny bungalow necessitated turning part of the basement into a family room. My dad and I installed a faux drop ceiling over it using pieces of scrounged drywall and wire coat hangers. When a local grocery store was going to discard a dozen lidded, corrugated cardboard boxes used to ship eggs ("egg crates"), my dad took them and painted them with leftover house paint. Then, once again using scrounged 2x4s, he built shelves for them in the basement. Convenient, inexpensive storage!

My mother did her part as well. No food was ever wasted. Instead it was put into carefully rinsed-out recycled food jars. I remember that an entire kitchen cabinet was filled with various sizes of empty, lidded glass jars, ready to accept any amount of food leftovers. Cooking grease was saved in empty cans and taken to a local convent, where the nuns made it into soap. Burned-out incandescent light bulbs were saved and taken to the local electric utility, where they were recycled. (!)

Some of the wood my dad used in his projects was left over from building the garage in our backyard. When my parents bought our house, they had a 2½ car garage built. Now that I think about it, I'm not sure why—we only owned one family car. But with five kids, we sure had a lot of bikes and other paraphernalia. At any rate, my scavenging forays soon filled more than half of the space. The whole time I was growing up, we were never able to fit more than one car in the 2½ car garage—even when later we collectively owned four or five cars. I recycled the junk that I scavenged into dozens of projects. Among them were a three-level treehouse with hinged trapdoors, a stage for putting on plays (I could nearly always supply the props), and various kid-powered vehicles.

Today, urban alleys are mostly gone. And suburban housing developments never had them. But the tradition of urban foraging still continues, albeit in a more sedate manner. The night before trash pickup day, pickup trucks can be seen slowly cruising down suburban streets (where more disposable income leads to more disposable goods), their drivers eyeing—and often picking up—the larger durable items that don't fit in the city-provided trash bins.

Local sanitation workers have shared with me stories of the treasures that they have taken home rather than to the dump. In fact, if I have anything repairable or that can still be used, I put it out at the end of the driveway on the weekend, and it is gone by trash day. I confess that I have done my share of foraging as well, picking up usable shelves, cabinets, chairs, tables, luggage, etc. I just can't bear to send to the landfill anything that can still be used.

We have curbside recycling in the city where I live now. At the outset of the program, each household was given two bins—

one for glass and plastic, and one for cardboard and newspaper. Yet few of my neighbors use them. When they saw how assiduously we recycled, a number of them gave their bins to us. With a family of six (or eight or ten when our kids' friends are staying with us), we typically have 7 or 8 bins filled with recycling and just two bags of trash. All of our food waste is composted in the garden. My parents' frugality lives on!

But of course today it is more than frugality—it is earthkeeping. I keep trying to convince my neighbors and my students that you can't really throw anything away because there is no *away*—all we've got is this one blue marble floating in space and we have to figure out how to sustain it. As van der Ryn and Cowan observe: "If we are to create a sustainable world—one in which we are accountable to the needs of all future generations and all living creatures—we must recognize that our present forms of agriculture, architecture, engineering, and technology are deeply flawed. To create a sustainable world, we must transform these practices."[64]

Until recently the energy efficiency of an automobile was not the major consideration of the American when making a choice. The Industrial Age's love of speed and power is embodied in the car that can accelerate from zero to sixty miles per hour in the shortest number of seconds possible. Why does any car have the capability of reaching the speed of 120 mph or more when the maximum speed limit is 70 mph? Fast cars, "muscle cars", big cars, sexy cars are the mechanical extension of our self-image and esteem. In many ways the car we choose is the physical manifestation of our values—both cultural and personal.

Matt's Story

I think that is true for me…I drive a Prius.

The energy efficient Prius has a screen in the middle of the dashboard that allows one to monitor the operation of the vehicle. On one screen you can track the direction of energy flow of the hybrid system. It's a lot of fun to see the arrows switching from the gasoline-powered engine to the battery and back. The hybrid engine is an example of the type of total systems thinking that we must all adopt for an energy efficient, low entropy future. The flow direction on the screen depends on whether you are accelerating, slowing or braking. By rethinking all the energy available in a moving vehicle engineers figured out how to capture the braking energy and store it in a battery for later use.

After driving for awhile you figure out that your driving habits have a significant effect on the energy efficiency of the vehicle—and then it becomes a game. The screen in the middle of the dashboard is pretty distracting when it comes to safe driving—but for me (and many others, I bet) it is the ultimate video game, meeting the real world. The efficiency measurement is in the form of miles per gallon and is shown on screen through a constantly changing statistical number and bar graph that bobs up and down. The challenge is to keep the bar as high as possible for as long as possible while driving.

You learn pretty quickly that pressing on the gas pedal is an immediate drop in efficiency—and accelerating from a standstill is the worst. I love playing this game. The best I've ever done is 60 miles per gallon over a 120 mile trip. There is a certain *zen* about driving a Prius. A friend says that you must drive as if you have an eggshell under the accelerator pedal.

After sitting at a traffic light (a position I try to avoid whenever possible), those around me zoom off when the light changes green. Irritated drivers pass around me as I slowly build up speed. In the game I play with my Prius I'm striving for maximum efficiency while those other folks are driven (and driving) to reach destinations in the shortest time. Who wins? I think I do.

The realization is that speed is not always equivalent to efficiency. In physics this is termed the "principle of least action." It's a very simple idea but with far-reaching consequences. Basically, it states that Nature always finds the most efficient course from one point to another. The orbits of planets, the path of a thrown ball, the path of a photon of light—all these will follow (of their own 'volition' it seems) paths of least action defined as paths in which the total energy needed to get from point A to point B is minimized. In other words, the shortest distance between two points is not always a direct line. In the Green Age the principle of least action will be a value beyond physics and mathematical calculation. It will be applied to all aspects of human management and decision making. It is the essential component of a Green Age ethic of conservation by which we must change our cultural priorities.

In the Industrial Age we value time. We are slaves to time. We are obsessed with time. We keep time, mark time, and strive to make time. We watch the clock, beat the clock and punch the clock. It is no coincidence that the invention and perfection of the clock parallels the growth and development of the Industrial Age. Somewhere along the way we made the transition from marking our activities through the rise and fall of the sun, to the click of the stopwatch secondhand. In this age dominated by measurement, it is the measurement of time that dominates us. We hang it on our walls, sit it on our desks, position it next to our beds, strap it to our wrists, and carry it around in the Apps on our cell phones. And how does that serve to sustain us? How does it serve in the living practice of sustaining the Earth?

In the Green Age, that values sustaining the earth and uses the principle of least action as a problem solving methodology, the concept of time is transformed. Efficiency is newly defined as the solution that requires the least energy transfer—time is no longer the ruling component. Time cannot be measured in the slices of ephemera that we humans have artificially constructed. Time is the eco-system's ability to recycle waste and renew stock of resources.

The Second Law of Thermodynamics is therefore also the real determinant of time. As we have discussed, in accordance with that law, energy flows – but only in one direction, from the usable to the unusable. If we consider what is really essential to humans, is time really only the tracking of planetary revolutions and orbits about the sun? In an age that values sustainability, Time exists only when there is energy flow. For us that means beneficial energy flow that enhances human lives. In the Green Age we know that we are the time keepers, guardians, protectors. We will keep time by using resources at their pace of regeneration. And we will sustain the earth and ourselves by doing that.

There is also great irony that we have an Industrial Age value in which we transform non-renewable resources into plastic objects that are short-term and disposable. The reality is that while we may use them for a short amount of time before sending them off to the landfill—the life span of these objects is anything but short term. Plastic does not biodegrade because it is a combination of elements extracted from crude oil, then re-mixed by chemists in white coats. These combinations are man-made and therefore are not subject to the processes of nature. Stated simply, they don't break down. However, plastic does rip, tear and break into smaller pieces. This process is called degrading. This can take centuries, depending on the type of plastic and the environmental conditions surrounding it. Plastic never really returns to the store of available resources. It just continues to degrade until it is plastic dust. In terms of human life on Earth, it lasts forever.

The Green Age will place a high value on the appropriate use of resources that cannot be replaced within any reasonable time frame of human existence – like petroleum. On the other hand, there will be a value on the natural rate of deterioration of materials as a primary determinant of planning and design. I sometimes ask my students to tell me the life span of a building. Answers are usually given in the 100's of years. The reality is that the life expectancy of the buildings we currently construct is about 40-50 years. Sure, we can all point to exceptions: The Pyramids, the Colosseum, the great Cathedrals, or even some buildings, neighborhoods, and whole cities in this country. But we know them *because* they are exceptions.

In the Green Age, sustainability is defined as transformation within the natural flows of energy—from order to disorder and from the usable to the unusable. The value of the Green Age placed on natural energy flow will produce a built environment of planned obsolescence. And that will be a good thing because the planning includes the return of resources to the available energy pool.

One of the great things about engineers is that they love to solve problems. What we are discovering is that ingenuity has a price. An Industrial Age value is to create "time saving" electronic gizmos that run themselves. They turn on, turn off, wake up, record our entertainment, make coffee, and (sort of) have an electronic parallel universe to our daily activities. Most of these activities are not really saving all that much time. It has become a classic generational joke that our children are the only ones who really know how to set all those timers.

How ironic that current checklists of energy and dollar saving strategies report that all of our electronic helpers are really adding to our utility bills. Many VCRs, televisions, kitchen appliances, computers and stereos with little glowing lights and digital clocks continue to draw power even when you think they are switched off. These have been named "phantom loads." According to the Department of Energy (DOE), up to 75 percent of the electricity used to power home electronics in the average household is wasted sending power to products that are turned off. Consumers are advised to use power strips and remember to switch them to "off." So the "time savers" have now created another requirement of "work" to our daily routine. Or, we could engineer another solution to solve this problem that we have created for ourselves.

Greg Hood, founder of GreenSwitch LLC, says his product is meant to fix the phantom load problem. GreenSwitch sends a radio signal to companion components in outlets around the home, taking the energy-saving idea of a power strip to a whole-house level. "Customers have the peace of mind knowing that all of those energy hogs typically left on will be turned off at the flip of a switch as they leave the house," says Hood. The system is expandable. For example, a package of eight light switches or outlets, a master switch and a programmable thermostat would cost less than $900! If you feel comfortable changing out a light switch, the installation is easy; however, a national installation service is available.

Or maybe we should just manufacture and use appliances that have simple on/off switches?

Matt's Story

When I was a young architect I spent several years working for a large Chicago architectural firm. I was lucky enough to be part of a four person team responsible for developing the construction details for projects to be built in Algeria. It was an unusual requirement of the project for that time—and even now—that the details for construction had to be limited to the skills of the local labor forces and limited to use primarily locally available materials. This was a design where less really was more. It was culturally appropriate architecture that improved the lives of the people in timeframes both short term and long term. It was an important lesson for an architect.

British economist Dr. Fritz Schumacher coined the term "Appropriate Technology" in his book, *Small is Beautiful—Economics as If People Mattered*[65], which is still the foundational text on a sustainable future. Schumacher was a respected economist who worked with John Maynard Keynes and John Kenneth Galbraith. For twenty years he was the Chief Economic Advisor to the National Coal Board in the United Kingdom. He opposed neo-classical economics by declaring that single-minded concentration on output and technology was dehumanizing. He held that one's workplace should be dignified and meaningful first, and efficient second. He also believed that nature (and the world's natural resources) is priceless.

Appropriate technology is the kind of technology that fits small-scale, community-centered economics: technology as if people mattered. According to Schumacher, Mother Nature never heard of "standardization." That is a concept from an economic world where people don't matter, except perhaps as workers and consumers. Appropriate technology has to fit the infinite variety of life on Earth, rather than forcing life to fit the technology. What this means for the built environment, both in infrastructure and architecture is a greater level of stylistic diversity based on local materials, climate and culture. These are the problems needing to be solved by engineers.

The "growth value" of the Industrial Age is expansion without limits. This includes the righteousness of conquest, and colonization that has extended from global exploration to the corporate boardroom. Darwin's theory of evolution, wherein only the fittest survive and prosper, has been applied as the model for business. It is justification for corporate aggressiveness and continued "no limits" use of resources. It is the underlying value that makes us want and acquire so much "stuff."

There is a satirical saying that gently mocks our cultural materialism and succinctly states the Industrial Age values of growth and acquisition:

"Whoever dies with the most toys –WINS!"

In the book: *Enough: True Measure of Money, Business and Life* John Bogle[66] recounts a conversation between two of the great authors of the 20th century, Kurt Vonnegut and Joseph Heller. At a party Vonnegut asked Heller how it felt to know that the man across the room had probably made more money in a day than Heller made from his book, *Catch 22*, during all the years it had been in print. Heller replied, "I have something he will never have—enough."

Schumacher also developed the concept of "enoughness," wherein the ideal is sufficiency, not surfeit. According to Schumacher, "Economic 'progress' is good only to the point of sufficiency, beyond that, it is evil, destructive, uneconomic."[67] Schumacher, who died in 1977, was a prophet of the Green Age. He understood that western economics measures standard of living by consumption, and therefore regards a person who consumes more as better off than one who consumes less. Schumacher argued that an economy should exist to serve the needs of people.

But in a materialist economy, people exist to serve the economy. Employers consider their workers to be "cost" that must be reduced as much as possible, and modern manufacturing uses production processes that require little skill. As evidence, he pointed to discussions among economists about whether full employment "pays," or whether some amount of unemployment might be better "for the economy." Modern economic practice, Schumacher wrote, "…is standing the truth on its head by considering goods as more important than people and consumption as more important than creative activity. It means shifting the emphasis from the worker to the product of work, that is, from the human to the subhuman, a surrender to the forces of evil."[68]

Schumacher's alternative is the idea of "enoughness," or providing what is sufficient. Instead of ever-increasing consumption, he argues that the emphasis should be on meeting human needs with no more consumption than is necessary. He also wrote that labor should be about more than production. Work has both psychological and spiritual value to human beings, and these should be treated with respect.

We have inherited an economic system that propels itself by stoking desire and reinforcing the notion that acquiring things will make us happier. We have no end of entertaining consumer products that soon end up in landfills, but we fail to provide for some basic human needs—like clean water, air, education, health care for each person.

In the Green Age enough is enough.

Enough stuff that is. But we can never have enough knowledge or information. The Green Age will be an Age of Knowledge. Anthropologist William Ury suggests that humanity is on the brink of a Knowledge Revolution, one whose effects will be every bit as profound as those of the Agrarian and Industrial Revolutions. Unlike land and factories, which are improved by possession, knowledge is improved by sharing, he observes. Consider the practice of modern science, in which knowledge is produced and refined through global information sharing.

Knowledge, moreover, is fundamentally democratic. Theoretically anyone can obtain it, and modern technology makes it easy to share. Pyramids collapse into networks, and old hierarchies are therefore undermined. Consider the rapid changes occurring in China today. Despite persistent government attempts at censorship, information and knowledge from outside continues to deluge the country. And an increasingly educated population spreads it through social networks.

"The Knowledge Revolution thus offers us perhaps the most promising opportunity in ten thousand years to create a 'co-culture' of coexistence, cooperation, and constructive conflict."[69] And, we might add, a democratic culture of sustainability, in which knowledge and practices of how to nurture the earth and its inhabitants spreads rapidly around the globe.

The Green Age will be an Age of Knowledge.

Chapter 9:
Green Age Worldview—Part Two

What then are the beliefs of the Green Age? To start with, the value of Stewardship is the essential human raison d'être. "Stewardship," say van der Ryn and Cowan, is quite different from management: it requires wisdom, restraint, and, above all, a commitment to and understanding of a particular place."[70] The particularity of place is central to a Green Age worldview. Essentially, all life forms are rooted in, and dependent on, place to survive, a point made by Winifred Gallagher in *The Power of Place:*. "Whether we listen to biologists describe the feedback between the cell and its milieu or psychologists discuss the fit between certain people and places, their words resonate with what ecologists say about the way the whole natural world works. At any level we can think of, ignoring our relationship with our environment puts both of us in jeopardy."[71]

We know that science and technology cannot solve all of our problems and in the Green Age, efficiency is defined as the solution that requires the least energy transfer. We understand that everything is connected to everything else to such a degree that if we destroy any part of nature, it affects all other parts, including human beings.

In the Industrial Age we believe that technology and nature are independent and unconnected. In the Green Age we understand that they are irrevocably connected and that the planet is a single organism. Because of this, we believe that our natural resources require public guardianship.

We believe the future is preserved in the actions we take today.

What kind of actions would we expect of our larger societal institutions, like corporations, agriculture, and education? We'll use the value of *sustaining the Earth as a whole system that supports human life* to see what we would expect in each area.

"Education," says David Orr, "is not widely regarded as a problem, although the lack of it is. The conventional wisdom holds that all education is good, and the more of it one has, the better....The truth is that without significant precautions, education can equip people merely to be more effective vandals of the earth."[72] The antidote to this is to use the value of sustaining the Earth as a whole system that supports human life as a rubric at every grade and in every subject that is taught.

Learning to think ecologically would literally change the way we look at everything we do. The value of sustaining the Earth would be so embedded in the way that we think, our feelings, and the actions that we take, that all of life would change in that direction. We envision a change as pervasive as the one that was created in our culture by having a world wide web integrated into our everyday lives. Our websites, blogs, e-mails, and Facebook pages are read by people from other countries and cultures around the world every day.

All economic activity is an extension of the environment; therefore, consumption is consciously tempered by the eco-system's ability to recycle waste and renew stocks of resources. We know that work is essential—as necessary for proper life balance as sleep, contemplation, or play. Without work, we human beings are incomplete. In the Green Age we believe that we ought to be able to find both dignity and purpose in the doing of our work.

Looking at corporations is made easier for us because work has already been done in this area. A term many of us may be familiar with is the "triple bottom line" (TBL). That phrase was generated by John Elkington in 1994.[73] Briefly, it means that we would no longer use an income statement's net profit as the single measure of whether a company is successful or not. Instead, the company would be measured on three standards as to its success. In addition to profit, the other two measures are ecology and society.

In order to be regarded as successful, the net bottom line must reflect that the stakeholders (present and future inhabitants of the Earth), not just shareholders, are benefitting from the continued operation of a business. Financial profit would also have to include all real costs of production. Throughout the Industrial Age, real costs of production have not included things like cleaning up messes that are toxic to the environment and consequently, to people and other biologically based organisms with whom we share this Earth.

What that means practically is that in order to succeed on the ecological bottom line, all of the processes, systems, flows, and material consumption must do no harm to the ecology of the Earth. Mined resources would only be able to be taken at the same rate that they could replenish themselves. Electric companies that sell energy funded primarily from burning coal, now sell that energy to consumers very inexpensively. But under this TBL measure, they would be responsible for cleaning the atmosphere of the excess carbon exhausted from their operating processes, and that cost would be passed along to the consumer. (We don't currently have a way of cleaning excess carbon from the atmosphere.)

In actuality, if the real costs of using coal were included in the financial bottom line of electric companies, coal would no longer be cheap energy. In this new way of thinking, electric companies would also only be able to take coal from the Earth at the same rate at which the coal could replenish itself. They would be forced to move into mining only renewable resources to generate energy—that is, from the sun, wind, and from flowing water.

The third measure of a business's success in TBL is society. This is a difficult measurement to take because it can be so subjective. The Global Reporting Initiative (GRI) has tried to address the subjective quality of reporting and measurement by establishing a set of guidelines.[74] Essentially, the guidelines are based on universal standards that are recognized internationally and on United Nations human rights declarations. The GRI reporting guidelines for social performance "concerns the impacts an organization has on the social systems within which it operates" and reviews performance practices of labor, "human rights, society, and product responsibility."[75]

We all may be familiar with some current examples of problems that have been identified in this area during recent years. One was the discovery by a U.S. clothing label whose manufacturing process took place in another country. The company discovered that child labor was being used in workhouses. Another recent example concerning product responsibility is the case in which a U.S. toy company, whose manufacturing took place in China, discovered that the paint used on its toys contained lead. Young children chew on toys, and when children ingest lead, they get sick. All the toys had to be recalled.

In the Green Age, the value of sustaining the Earth would lead us to expect that all companies exhibit success at each of these levels. Financially, companies must include all costs of doing business in the computation of their net profit. Ecologically, they must ensure that all of their systems, processes, materials use, and product distribution do no harm to the Earth or its resources. And socially, they must show that they honor human rights through their labor practices, and through their production of goods that do not harm people.

Next we'll use the value of *sustaining the Earth as a whole system that will support human life* to look at agriculture. What would we expect from companies that grow food? How would companies that grow food sustain the Earth as a whole system? In an earlier chapter, we talked about what agriculture has become during the recent past. We have corporations that farm and grow food in various parts of the country, then ship the goods to central distribution warehouses, and from there goods are shipped to the entire United States. This method uses approximately 18,400 BTU's of energy to produce one dollar of output. The agricultural yield per acre is roughly the same as can be produced by local organic farms, but the transportation required increases the non-renewable energy used. This existent method of food production and delivery is extremely inefficient and costly for both the planet and present and future stakeholders.

In using this value of *sustaining the Earth* to determine what we would expect from companies that grow our food, we would require them to use resources at the rate at which they can renew themselves. We also would require that the air we breathe is not fouled, the water we drink is not put at risk, and that the crops and end products have a nutritional value that is high enough to support healthy human life. That eliminates the use of fossil fuels almost entirely. We would require that whatever they use to fertilize would make the soil more fecund, and the food that grows from that soil, more nutritious.

Fecal matter from animals, as well as pesticides and herbicides, regularly make their way into the water tables, ponds, streams, and rivers. Because of that, we would also want any pesticides to be natural pest enemies, and natural herbicidal measures rather than chemical. These requirements also mean that food production and distribution would have to become localized. It has worked in the past; it can work again.

Finally we'll use the value of *sustaining the Earth as a whole system that will support human life* to mean supporting human community.

Pat's Story

As a child of the Baby Boom generation, I grew up with a lot of other kids. In fact, when I was in elementary school, I counted nearly 100 other children living on my two-block-long

103

city street. And almost all of them played at our house! My brothers and sister and I each had our extended cohort of friends that sometimes played separately, sometimes together at our house. The attraction was partly physical—we had that garage filled with wonderful junk, a treehouse, and a wiffleball diamond I created in the backyard using half-buried bundles of rags for bases.

But the attraction was social, too. Most moms in the neighborhood were stay-at-home moms, but our mom seemed to be the most friendly and tolerant. Looking back, I don't know how my mom managed to consistently feed peanut butter sandwiches and Kool Aid to so many kids. My dad worked on straight commission, and some weeks dinners were pretty lean in the days before payday. But my mom always came through for the kids.

My dad was a huge supporter as well. His Irish wit and love of children so enchanted our friends that they would watch for him to come home in the evening. As his car turned the corner at the end of our street, dozens of kids would drop what they were doing and run toward it, shrieking "Daddio! Daddio!" (a nickname I had given him after he explained beatniks to me). My dad would then pack all the kids in the car (this was before seatbelts) and give us a ride around the block. Sometimes he drove an extra block to the local Dairy Queen and bought us all nickel cones. (Years later my mother told me that Dad often spent his lunch money for the entire week doing this.) I have no idea what the other parents in the neighborhood thought about this, but I knew that all the kids loved my parents and loved playing at our house.

One of the neighbors across the street was an unmarried man who lived with his mother. This man was a fanatic about his lawn. He spent all his free time trimming, fertilizing, watering, and even regularly replacing his postage-stamp-sized lawn. Obviously his lawn was quite a contrast to ours, which was worn with the traffic and play of dozens of kids.

One summer when I was about 14, I was outside working on some project with my dad when this neighbor came over and announced that "some of the neighbors" were concerned with the shabby state of our lawn. Without hesitating, my dad looked him in the eye and said, in a perfectly friendly but matter-of-fact voice, "Well, you see, right now I'm not raising grass, I'm raising kids." Nothing more was said; the man walked away and we went on with our project. But that moment deeply affected me. I felt valued. And I was so proud of my dad for sticking up for us kids, and valuing people over stuff.

Yes, we need more people like my dad. But more importantly we need communities that grow and develop people like this—communities that are nurturing, that see people as assets, and help to sustain social life. In their acclaimed work *Habits of the Heart,* Robert Bellah et al. note that such communities give us "the sense of growing up in a morally and intellectually intelligible world."[76] This is not a paean to a remembered 1950s world that really never was. Rather, it is a call to build a future on timeless principles of sociality, harking all the way back to our millenia-old Hunter-Gatherer roots.

Part Six: Transform!

In Part Six, we look at how we are to make the personal changes that are necessary to make the way in which we live sustainable. We investigate what actions we will need to take both personally and socially in order to live a sustainable life, as well as how to live with a conscious eye toward the fact of the second law of thermodynamics as a basic understanding—something that we use to make our choices in the lives that we live. We identify the roadblocks we encounter on the way to making change, and investigate processes that assist us in moving through those roadblocks.

We tell stories of transformation—identifying ways in which we have made changes in our lives, and give practical solutions—steps that you can follow to live your life more consciously and make choices that will sustain the Earth.

Chapter 10:
Glimmers of Change-Making

> "Be the change you wish to see in the world."
> Mahatma Gandhi

What do we need to do to make a difference for life on Earth? How do we make the personal changes that are necessary to make the way we live sustainable? Unless we experience total societal collapse, we are not going to return to the Hunter-Gatherer stage of human existence. Nor are we going to move backward in time to the Agrarian Age. What actions will we need to take both personally and socially in order to transform our industrial society into a sustainable one? And how do we live with a conscious eye toward the fact of the Second Law of Thermodynamics as a basic understanding—something that we use to make our choices in the lives that we live?

How do you live your life? Most of us are shaped by the ideas of the past that dominate the institutions of the present and predetermine how we react to them. We are inevitably stuck with one foot in the past while we are often frantically reacting to the events of the present. We all know intellectually that change is inevitable, yet we do nothing to address what may be coming.

Edgar Mitchell, the sixth man to walk on the moon, has provided a vision for the future. His vision is that

> the third millennium will bring a new dawn of awareness such that the genius and creativity which we exhibit as individuals will be harnessed together in concert, globally, to resolve the problems which we have unwittingly collectively created and which threaten existence as we know it. This vision cannot

possibly become reality without each of us, as he or she awakens to the dilemma, to first make a personal decision to live life productively toward creating a sustainable civilization for all, then to reach beyond our personal commitment to self and family to assist others also to recognize that our cultural traditions have created the crisis and must be re-examined.[77]

What we propose in this book is for you to become a person of the future—a member of what Thomas Friedman calls the "Re-Generation."[78] Can you create a personal vision of the future, incorporating new values and beliefs? When you take that action and become a person with a strong future vision, your daily actions begin to follow. Your personal vision will lead you to continual growth, creating, modifying and transforming your world (and the world). With a strong future vision you automatically set goals to create a life of purpose, growth and adventure. Your sphere of influence will begin to affect the actions that others take as well.

Do you want to be a leader in the effort to make the Earth contain a brighter future for those who will inherit—our children and grandchildren? Have you made the decision to change? In order to answer this you will need to look inside of yourself for the honest answers. Many people decide to make changes in their lives, but few meet with success. All that we have to do is look at the number of failed diets and New Year's resolutions for evidence. There is a big difference between deciding to do something and having the ability and determination to carry through and actually do it. What are your reasons for entering the Green Age? Do you know yourself and why you make the decisions you do in your life?

As we awaken to an understanding of the unsustainability of our world as we know it, there is also an undeniable sense of loss, frustration and confusion about where to go from this point. In 1969 the psychiatrist Elisabeth Kübler-Ross, M.D. published the groundbreaking book, *On Death and Dying*.[79] It describes, in five discrete stages, a process by which people deal with grief and tragedy. Kübler-Ross originally applied these stages to people suffering from terminal illness, and later to any form of catastrophic personal loss. Our planet is suffering. Our world view is shattered. We need to grieve. It's worth taking a moment to examine the Kübler-Ross model, especially as it relates to the process people need to follow to make meaningful changes in their personal lives and in society.

Stage one: Denial — "I feel fine." "This can't be happening—not to me." "Surely things are not as bad as they seem." Denial is usually only a temporary defense for the individual and much of our society is still in this stage. Many who "have the microphone" continue to declare that the status quo must continue and that the actions of human beings have no deleterious effect on the environmental conditions of our planet. Since it is difficult for individuals to fully grasp global processes and problems, it seems easier to just ignore them and hope that they will go away—or at least won't have too adverse an effect on us.

Stage two: Anger — "Why me/us? It's not fair!" "How can this happen to me/us?" "Someone must be to blame – and they have to pay!" "I'm mad as hell about what they are doing to our planet!" According to the Kübler-Ross Model in the second stage, there is a recognition that denial cannot continue. Because of these feelings of anger, others may experience the person as difficult. In the case of global warming, against whom is our anger directed? Some folks direct it toward those who are doing nothing to make change; others direct it toward those who are taking action that may help to curb the condition. But after the rush of emotion associated with the anger subsides, there is the potential of a lapse into apathy.

Stage three: Bargaining —"I'll do anything for a few more years." "I will give my life savings if..." "Maybe if I do just this one thing...." The third stage involves the hope that the individual can somehow postpone or delay death. Usually, the

111

negotiation for an extended life is made with a higher power in exchange for a reformed lifestyle. The worldview we've all been living from tells us that technology will fix everything. We bargain that technological advances will maintain our growth and prosperity without provoking any fundamental changes. We presume that allowing "clean" industries to sell carbon offsets to "dirty" ones is making progress on the problem of pollution, or we feel righteous about buying electric cars without looking at the issue of electric power generation by fossil fuels.

We have just moved through a time in which we've seen massive greed at its worst in the United States. The greed of the chief executive officers of some of our largest corporations, together with the fact that Wall Street regulations had been removed by the actions of our government, wreaked havoc on our economy. Socially, we have allowed the people in charge of our money—our savings, mortgages, and retirement accounts— to pillage the system (us) for all that it was worth, and make off with billions of dollars. We adults, constituting the American public, are left with the bill.

We have bailed out these large corporations, whose leaders have made exorbitant sums of money, because so many of our livelihoods—our jobs—have depended on the viable continuance of those businesses. In effect, we are the ones who've paid these fellows to make off with our money, and we're left wringing our hands and wondering how in the heck we could prevent that from happening again! So we elected a new President, one who realizes the folly of removing Wall Street regulations, and has subsequently replaced them, in an effort to regain some sense of security and improve the health of our economy.

Stage four: Depression — "I'm so sad, why bother with anything?" "We are all going to die . . . What's the point in trying to change or fix anything?" "The problems seem so overwhelming...." "We've screwed things up so badly, they can't really be fixed." During the fourth stage, people begin to understand the inevitability of the irreversible processes we have set in motion. And, they may believe, nothing can be done. Because of this, individuals may become silent. In the context of our movement toward a Green Age, the individual may take the attitude of "Why bother, nothing I do is going to make any difference anyway."

Stage five: Acceptance — "It's going to be okay." "I can't fight it, I may as well prepare for it." "I will accept my share of the responsibility for the problem—and for creating the solution." This final stage comes with peace and understanding. In our transformation to the Green Age we will establish an internal personal commitment to live life productively and do our part to create a sustainable civilization for all.

Changing direction is hard. Just ask any sailor who is changing course to head into the prevailing wind. It is much easier to "go with the flow." As parents and counselors we talk to students about avoiding "peer pressure." When we go against the prevailing worldview, we are the recipients of ultimate levels of peer pressure. The entire world is set to flow in one direction with its precepts and values ingrained in us form birth. Yet we intellectually know we need to take a different path.

It is important to think about how to make two different kinds of internal changes. One is to make change in the face of addiction; and the other is to make change in the face of habit. Both kinds of change are difficult to make, and neither can be made by the intellect alone. We can understand, for example, that smoking is bad for us, but that understanding doesn't necessarily mean that we stop smoking. We must engage other aspects of ourselves in order to make the change that's needed.

Pat's Story

When I was in graduate school, we lived in an apartment complex at the edge of the developed area of our college town. The area around our apartment buildings was as-yet-undeveloped woodland and field. The residents of the apartments were all students or young professionals. We would gather in the halls at the end of the day and joke, laugh, complain, and share our plans for the future. Some of us walked our dogs through the surrounding fields, which gave us an intimate appreciation of nature.

Over one winter we discussed how nice it would be to have a garden nearby. Some were motivated by the desire to reconnect with the natural world that they had known growing up, and some were attracted mostly by the prospect of saving precious money. Since nearly everyone in my building was enthusiastic about the idea, I contacted the owners of the land. It was the energy crisis of the 1970s, so there were no plans to develop the land anytime soon, and the owners were amenable to letting us garden. None of us had any equipment, so we got a local farmer to plow some of the open ground. Since he couldn't plow a bunch of tiny plots with a tractor, he wound up plowing about a quarter acre. We had a community garden!

The land hadn't been farmed in a long time, and it wasn't very good—mostly heavy clay. I immediately bought a number of books about organic gardening and took out a subscription to *Organic Gardening* magazine (praise Robert Rodale!). We established a community compost pile to provide fertilizer and improve the tilth of the soil. We used natural mulch from the surrounding fields. We shared ideas and worked out solutions to problems. Sometimes we asked questions of knowledgeable people at the university.

Soon we began to harvest the bounty of the land. One couple bought a freezer, which they let others use. The rest of us shared canning equipment. By the Fall, my wife and I had about 6 dozen jars of vegetables, tomato sauce, and gazpacho. We shared harvest feasts in the halls of our apartment building and at the community center.

When we moved to our present city, we had a near impossible wish list: a house near the university (so that I could bike to work) with land for gardening and a south-facing exposure so that we could have a solar room. Amazingly, we found just such a location. Near the university was a typical 1950s-era suburban housing addition. The lots were rather large—about a half acre—and, amazingly, no one had put up fences around their backyards. The small ranch house was not terribly attractive, but it did have a southern exposure. At the back of the lot, woods ran east-west for a half-mile or so. Next door, an unimproved lot was mostly wooded.

But in typical suburban fashion, the house was surrounded by lawn. Previous owners had even mowed beyond the boundaries of the lot to increase the lawn area. The first time we mowed, it took *seven hours* behind a push mower! We immediately began building a dozen raised garden beds in the backyard. We planted ground cover on the east and west sides of the house, and let the woods encroach into the yard from two sides. We sunk an old bathtub in the backyard to make a pond and created brush piles in the woods to provide cover for small animals. A compost pile recycles lawn and garden waste as well as food scraps. (We seem to share it with raccoons.) We have planted numerous trees and created additional natural areas around our lot. Our exceedingly shrunken lawn now takes about an hour and a half to mow. (We only mow the areas used for sports and social activities.)

We added a solar room to the back of the house, complete with heat-retaining tiles, thermal curtains, and a wood stove. A large lean-to in the yard stores wood for the stove, a great deal of which is harvested from our land. We bought half of the lot next door so that it can never be built on and the woods (and associated fauna) can flourish. With the energy-efficient windows and expanded insulation we added to the house, we can heat it entirely with the wood stove.

We added a large deck so that we can enjoy the bounty of nature in our backyard. In the expanded woods there are deer, red fox, rabbits, raccoons of course and the occasional skunk family. Bats and a variety of songbirds live in the woods. At the top of the food chain, hawks are frequent visitors as well.

The social and community aspects have not been neglected. The remaining lawn area in the backyard is a soccer pitch, complete with a full-size goal. There is also an above-ground pool, heated with a passive solar heater that I built. We designed and built a jungle gym in the backyard. Because of our large lot and a deep setback from the road, we have a 75-foot paved driveway. Many neighborhood kids have learned to ride their bikes there. There is a basketball backboard and hoop; a portable net was used for roller hockey games, and various pipes and boards provided opportunities for grinding with skateboards.

And yes, hearkening back to my childhood, while growing up our children's friends and neighbors played at our house! We frequently had a dozen or more children hanging out. As I struggled to keep enough juice and snacks stocked, I wondered again how my mother had done it. We got involved with our neighborhood association and got to know both the neighbors and the neighborhood by volunteering for a citizens' security patrol one or two evenings a month.

This journey began with our simple desire to save money by growing some of our own vegetables, and our student-related poverty that induced us to find inexpensive ways to socialize. The journey evolved into educating ourselves about natural processes, and the complex interrelationships among flora and fauna in an ecological system. And then doing something – however small – about it. Gandhi said, "Almost anything you do will seem insignificant, but it is important that you do it." We can each take the steps that we can. We still keep in regular contact with some of the people from those community garden days, even though we live in different states.

Here are a few questions that will help you identify your reasons for entering the Green World:

How do you feel deep down inside?

Do you often wonder if you are on the right path?

What are the pros and cons of continuing in your current direction?

Would you like to create a brighter future?

When you answer these questions your reasons for making the decision to change will become clear. Be sure to write them down. You transform your life when reasons for change become goals. Can you list five important specific accomplishments you can make in the months to come?

The power of goal setting as a written exercise seems to be one of the great secrets of success. Benjamin Franklin knew the importance of writing down one's goals. Franklin placed great value on self-improvement. He believed that integrity and moral responsibility were the backbone of a successful life and a strong community. Reading and reflection led him to formulate his own list of 13 personal virtues, which he then attempted to master, one by one, noting his progress each day in a chart. This is similar to the life-changing method of goal setting described by Lou Holtz. Holtz is best known as the successful head football coach for the University of Notre Dame. He is a strong proponent of goal setting as daily motivation.

In 1966, Holtz, at 28 years of age was assistant coach at the University of South Carolina and had spent virtually every penny he had in the bank to make a down payment on a house. Holtz's wife, Beth, was eight months pregnant with the couple's third child when changes in South Carolina's football staffing meant that suddenly Holtz was unemployed. He was depressed, without direction and questioning whether he was in the right profession. He came across a book called *The Magic of Thinking*

Big by David Schwartz.[80] At that time in his life, Holtz says he was not motivated to do much of anything.

One of the directives in the book that he decided to act on was to write down every goal he wanted to achieve before he died. In the film "An American Family" he describes how he sat down at the dining room table, and let his imagination go. Before he knew it, he had listed 107 professional, parenting, and spiritual goals that he wanted to achieve in his life. One of the goals he wrote down that day was to become head football coach at Notre Dame. It seemed impossible, even ridiculous. But in 1986 he found himself in exactly that job. He went on to become one of Notre Dame's most successful coaches. He has also met the other 106 goals he set for himself, and continues to use goal setting as an essential part of his life structure.

Matt's Story

As a student in my early 20's I attended several colleges and universities until I finally got fed up with the feeling of being blown by the winds of fate. Education was important to me, but not all THAT important. Then I discovered architecture. I wanted to be successful, but was under-prepared and over-confident. My first year was a disaster. One professor suggested that I had not yet "found my niche." But I knew that I needed to take control of my life instead of reacting to the pressures of parental plans and social norms.

At the end of the semester I had to take stock and decide what I was going to do. It seems hokey now and seemed self-consciously odd then, but I sat down and wrote myself a letter. In it I informed myself that I was going to buckle down and get serious about this architecture stuff. The college spring trip to Chicago included a visit to the architecture firm of Skidmore Owings and Merrill. I included working at that firm as one of the goals in my letter to myself. I folded the letter, placed it in an envelope, and put it away. The next semester went better. I became close friends with several professors who mentored me through graduate school. I forgot about the letter and Skidmore Owings and Merrill as I strove to develop an architectural response to the energy crisis of the 1970's.

Then in the early 80's I found myself in the same predicament as Lou Holtz. My wife was eight months pregnant. The architect I was working for in Chicago was closing his office. It was November and I was desperate for a job. The economy was in a downturn and interest rates were soaring. No one was building and all the architecture firms were slowing down. I figured if anyone had a job it would be the big firms. So I found myself at the door of the largest firm in Chicago – Skidmore Owings and Merrill, and was told they too were not hiring. But the next day I got a phone call asking me to come in for an interview. It was a pleasant interview, but not too hopeful until the last question. Did I happen to speak French?

As it turned out I had taken a year of French as part of my undergraduate degree requirements. I also had passed the Graduate Record Exam in reading proficiency in French. Somehow life had provided me with the exact skills and experience needed for the only job they had available. The projects they were working on were located in Algeria. All the construction documents were to be noted in French. Is it a coincidence that I had written down a goal that later manifested itself in my life? I don't think so.

Chapter 11:
The Internal Process of Change-Making

What are the "rules" you follow unconsciously that shape your life? We all have them. We have patterns of behavior that rule how we eat, communicate, drive, parent—just about everything we do. What qualifies these rules is whether they bring us closer to, or push us further from our goals. If you have decided to enter into the Green Age worldview, then you need to take a look at the rules you hold. What four rules might prevent you from reaching your goals? What four new patterns of behavior do you need to establish to reach your goals?

In the world of design and construction there is a lot of talk about what it will take to create a built environment that is sustainable. The measurement of success can be reduced to four basic concepts. These qualities of sustainability can also be applied to our personal lives as a metric.

1. Understand that the earth is a finite system and is a model for making sustainable life decisions.

Our false mechanical world view is based on a premise of unlimited, inexhaustible resources. To live a sustainable life we look to the natural regenerative processes of the Earth. Creative designers and manufacturers have new interest in looking at biological systems in nature to see how similar problems are solved. On a daily basis we can reconnect to the pulse of the earth by setting daily rhythms to match those of nature. What are your eating habits? When do you sleep? How do you exercise?

2. Achieve a balance of resource use with the ability of systems to regenerate.

Where do we start? We simply can no longer allow making money to be the sole measure of success—not on an individual basis, and not on a corporate basis. When we make personal decisions based on this, we end up living soulless lives. When we make societal decisions based on this, we end up sacrificing all the qualities that nourish and sustain our culture. Can it include everything in existence and extend forward in time to future generations?

From the moment of our birth as individuals we are energy processors in accordance with the Second Law of Thermodynamics. Energy passes through us transforming from the usable to the unusable. Human beings need energy to survive—to breathe, move, pump blood—and they acquire this energy from food. Anyone who has ever thought about a diet knows that food is measured in calories. What does that mean? A calorie is a measurement of heat. The number of calories in a food is a measure of how much potential energy that food possesses.[81] To live in balance with energy flow each day we would consume the same number of calories we expend. Some of our food energy is stored as muscle, bone, and other tissues; otherwise, children would not grow, and athletes could not develop larger muscles. However, when we take in more calories than our metabolism can process, or that are used in growth, the excess is stored—and it is stored as fat!

In all of our interactions we are energy processors. Things pass through our lives as a continual flow of energy. We are always in one of three stages: Acquisition, Use, or Disposal. When we acquire more stuff than we can use in a reasonable amount of time it is stored—somewhere—usually in the attic, basement or in an overstuffed closet. Sometimes it is "stored" in a landfill, but it doesn't go away until it has finally reached the point where all of its "energy" is spent.

Some furniture designers are now considering what happens to a chair at the end of its useful life. Where does it go? How many of its parts can be returned to the resource pool?

How much of the stuff that passes through your life could be returned to the resource pool?[82]

3. Rely on natural energy flows

In design and construction the first method of sustainability is to reduce the initial embodied energy of a material. Initial embodied energy in new construction represents the non-renewable energy consumed in the acquisition of raw materials, their processing, manufacturing, transportation to site, and construction. Strategies include not using petroleum based products, or limiting our use to those that are manufactured nearby. We can use similar strategies in our daily life. Do we know how far the meat traveled to make the hamburger we got at the drive-up window under the big yellow **M**? What materials were used to make your clothes?

The second method of sustainability is to reduce recurring embodied energy. In the built environment, this is all the non-renewable energy consumed during the operation, maintenance, and repair of building components measured throughout the entire life of the building. A sustainable building is easy to maintain, is in harmony with its environment, and minimizes fuel use. Can we live a low maintenance life? A sustainable life is built around habits that promote health, longevity, and low maintenance.

4. Eliminate the concept of waste

We think of waste as the stuff in the garbage can that is heading out to the curb; however, that isn't the only place that we can find waste in our lives. We have waste in poor communication, unfit tools, ineffective processes, and unrealistic expectations. Review the goals and passions in your life. Everything that holds you back from what is important is potentially waste. If you create a list of ten things that get in the way of your goals and passions you will find the waste in your life. Eliminate it.

We've outlined the following steps to the internal process of making change occur—a list to satisfy the intellect.

Step 1: Feel the discomfort with the current circumstances.

Step 2: Visualize your intention. (I'm going to do…)

Step 3: Muster the will to do (I will.)

Step 4: Engage the creative/meditative level.

Step 5: Make a plan—small steps make a big difference.

Step 6: Set deadlines—a plan without a deadline is just a dream.

Step 7: Take action—personal first, then social.

Step 8: Periodically evaluate your effectiveness—to stay on track.

Regina's Story

In thinking about how I make change happen inside of me, I realized that when I make important change that sticks, there is a fairly specific method that I follow. First I feel a level of discomfort with the way things are. Let's face it—we rarely (if ever) make lasting change in our lives if we are completely comfortable with what is. Next, I envision what I would like. I ask myself the question of what I would passionately embrace. We have to imagine it and redefine ourselves in order for it to come into being. Then, I engage the creative/meditative aspect of myself by writing, journaling, drawing, painting, what that passion looks and feels like to me.

Using an activity to engage the creative/meditative internal mode of being is the most crucial part, yet it is the one we least often take the time to purposefully employ. In order to engage the creative aspect of ourselves, we have to allow the brain to move into a brain wave level that is slower, more peaceful. There are four measurable levels of brain wave activity: Beta, Alpha, Theta, and Delta. Brain waves are generated by the individual cells in the brain, called neurons, which communicate with each other by making electrical changes that make brain waves visible when we look at an EEG (electroencephalogram). They are measured in cycles per second (Hertz; Hz is the short form). The lowest number of Hz represents the slower frequency of brain activity, called Delta; while the highest Hz/frequency represents Beta level of brain activity.[83]

Beta level brain waves are those we usually operate from in our work-day world. We think and reason from this level, and although this brain wave level is capable of discerning a next step in a logical process, it is unlikely that anything new will be generated, as it doesn't have access to creative levels of thinking. From Beta brain wave levels, we make lists and resolutions, but real change is unlikely to occur.[84]

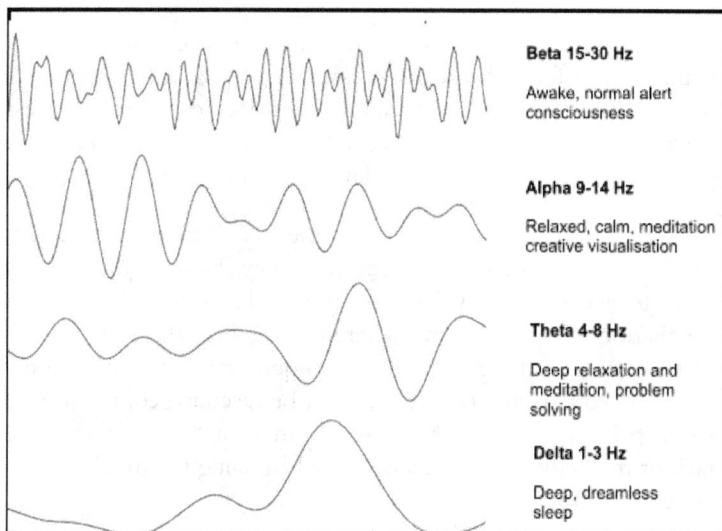

Beta 15-30 Hz

Awake, normal alert consciousness

Alpha 9-14 Hz

Relaxed, calm, meditation creative visualisation

Theta 4-8 Hz

Deep relaxation and meditation, problem solving

Delta 1-3 Hz

Deep, dreamless sleep

Alpha is the next deeper brain wave level. When this level is active in us we are creative, can see new ways of doing things, think out of the box, and make change that sticks. This is the level that Matt must have been in when he wrote his letter to himself. This brain wave will be naturally available to us as we are just moving into or out of sleep, but we can also take actions that purposefully activate the alpha brain wave level. We can directly access this level through meditation—there are many methods to try. Find one that works best for you. I long ago established an early morning meditation practice that I have found makes this creative brain wave level more easily accessible to me throughout the day.

If meditation isn't your bag, the alpha brain wave level can be engaged in other ways as well. Try a number of things: journaling—stream of consciousness writing or contour drawing without allowing the pen to leave the paper; drawing or painting—with the non-dominant hand; asking yourself a question to which you want a creative answer and then respond to the question by writing with your non-dominant hand; or discard your inhibitions and try moving to music in the way that it makes you feel. A friend accesses this alpha brain wave level when he's working on a machine in his workshop; runners access it when they engage in long runs. These are just a few ways that you can try to invoke the alpha level of brain waves.

Theta level brain waves are the most creative level that most of us can consciously access. I only know of a couple of ways to access this level purposefully. I begin each day with meditation. I've tried many different kinds over the years, and all of them work as long as I am able to quiet my mind and still my body. If you decide to try this, don't be discouraged if you have to keep bringing your mind back from your "to do" list. The task of meditation is often a continual bringing the mind back to stillness in the moment.

Another way to purposefully engage this brain wave level is one that gave Einstein one of his most famous solutions, "E=MC squared," and gave James Watson and Francis Crick the design of our DNA—Watson had a dream in which he imagined a series of spiral staircases. All you have to do is to think about a question or write it down before you go to sleep or take a nap, and ask your subconscious mind to work on the problem for you while you are asleep. Upon awakening, be aware of anything that is in your mind as you come to the surface. You can also keep a tablet by your bedside and write down any dreams that come to you in the night. This takes practice. Don't get discouraged if answers don't come right away—keep at it and you will realize the benefits of this practice.

The Delta brain wave level is our state of consciousness when we are in deep, dreamless sleep. I have read about some yogis who consciously engage in this level of brain wave (non-activity) without actually being asleep, but I haven't done it myself, so can't tell you how to get there. But we can accomplish change without accessing this delta brain wave level, so now we'll go on to the final step in my practice of making internal change that sticks. I take action on the passionate vision.

One change in the face of addiction that I have made was when I stopped smoking nearly thirty years ago. This is what that process looked like in action. The timeframe was 1979, and I was in my early thirties. My children, Troy and Gina, who were ten and seven years old at the time had both gone on a school outing to a local Health Center that day and had witnessed the graphically displayed innards of a body that smoked, and one that had not. They talked about it on the way home and came up with a plan of action.

When they walked in the door, they told me where they had been and what they had seen, and they both said that all they wanted for Christmas that year was for me to quit smoking. There was step one. I felt an extreme level of discomfort! My children weren't asking for toys for Christmas—they were asking me to quit smoking! Now I had to do it! Step two; envisioning what I wanted was planted firmly in my brain. I could see myself free from that addiction.

I learned at that time that it would take seven years for my lungs to recover from the damage inflicted by the inhalation of smoke. I also learned that if I would run, massive amounts of fresh air would be pumped into my lungs and the recovery time would be shortened. So my steps three and four, engaging the creative and meditating, was to journal about it each day—sometimes more than once. Journaling is both a creative and meditative process for me. Step five involved putting on a pair of running shoes every time I wanted a cigarette, and heading out the door. At first I could only run for about a block, but within a couple of weeks, I was running once a day, but for much longer distances.

Running also involved the activity of meditation, endorphins kick in and the alpha brain wave level is activated. While I ran, I redefined myself by repeating over and over in my mind: "I am not a smoker; I am a runner." By the end of two weeks, that's exactly the change that happened. I was no longer a smoker; I was a runner! I no longer craved a cigarette at all, and haven't wanted one since. Troy and Gina got their Christmas wish fulfilled (and toys too), and I have gained a healthier body and life.

This ability to move into the more creative alpha level brain wave can be achieved in many more ways involving strenuous physical activity. Distance running is just one way to do this. Others are swimming, bicycling, hiking in nature--anything that will stimulate enjoyment and cause you to lose yourself in the present moment.

This next part is the one with which I have the most trouble. Breaking habits! Habits are those mostly small, but sometimes large things that we do every day, and the sum of those parts make up a life. They are so automatic that they are difficult to see. Most of them aren't a problem; most are innocuous—they are things like making the bed automatically, or having two cups of coffee in the morning, or crossing the right leg over the left when you sit down to relax. Most aren't a problem; but some are.

One of the habits that I've developed in my life (and I know I have lots of company in this one), is eating my meals while I'm doing something else. I don't take the time to savor, experience the sensual, in the activity of eating. I may watch a television program or read, but I don't take the opportunity to enjoy my food and the activity of eating itself. Because I don't do that one thing by itself, I also don't notice when my stomach is feeling full. I don't notice when my body is telling me that it is time to stop feeding it. Usually it isn't until about twenty minutes after I'm done eating that I notice an uncomfortable feeling of fullness in my tummy. The irony is that when I'm on vacation, one of the most pleasurable things that I look forward to is the long and leisurely dinners, enjoyed with friends.

By now, in the United States we know that, as a population, we are overweight. We eat fast food in our cars, or bolt our lunches down at our desks. Enjoyment of our food is usually relegated to the "quick fix" of a candy bar from the gas station when we stop by to fill our tanks up, or a drive through at Dairy Queen for this month's featured "Blizzard," or we indulge in a quick salty treat in the form of a small bag of chips from the vending machine.

The idyllic meals that are depicted in Martha Stewart's magazine, with family and friends seated at a long country table on the (exquisitely manicured and spacious) lawn, just outside of everyone's backdoor, are the stuff of fantasy for most of us. If we do create those events, they occur about three or four times per year at holiday celebrations. We don't have time, make time, or take the time to enjoy our food. We eat so fast most of the time that we have things like Pepcid AC, Rolaids, and Tums on hand as after dinner mints! Even our relationships with folks are bolted down as quickly as our meals are—"r u kidng?—do u thnk we hv tm 2 sit dn on a lwn to eat?" "Jst txt me!"

So, what is the habit that I need to break here? Is it the one in which I eat mindlessly as I prepare for classes at my desk? Is it the one in which I value work more than personal time? As I think about this issue, one of the verbs that I've used in this writing keeps coming to the forefront of my mind, and that is "to savor." What would happen if I were to change my approach to daily life from being in "get 'er done" mode to "savoring" mode? As I write this, I realize how much I value and identify with that relentless work ethic that propels me through my day. The change that I need to make is the one in which I move from the mindless "get 'er done" mode to a mindful savoring—of each of life's moments. It needs to happen in many more areas of my life than just when I eat!

So, here is my first step—I feel a level of discomfort with the way things are. I don't like the feeling of being overfull, and not being able to do anything to prevent it by the time I notice. I am also uncomfortable with days going by without my having experienced any savoring at all. In my second step, I must envision what I would like—what is the vision that I would passionately embrace? I'll stick to my experience with food first, especially the times when I'm eating by myself, because that's when I tend to mindlessly bolt food down while I'm doing something "important." For example, this morning when I ate my breakfast—blueberries with yogurt—I ate mouthfuls while I got ready for work and packed the car. Today at lunch, I ate at my desk while reading and responding to e-mails. My new vision for all of my eating experiences is one that I can definitely embrace with passion.

One of my favorite sensual and savoring experiences of eating while alone was a lunch that I had in the middle of Acadia National Park. I had taken a restorative vacation to Maine by myself and went to the Jordan Pond Restaurant on Mount Desert Island in Acadia. The meal that I ate was simple, but the combination of the beauty of the location, immersed in nature, with the taste of the food was incredible.

As you can see from the pictures, the dining experience on this lawn, immersed in such a beautiful natural setting, could hardly be anything but wonderful. I ate lobster stew with freshly made, still warm popovers, and tea. Wait staff stopped by my table frequently to offer warm popovers. Jam pots of blueberry jam and honey, along with real butter were served with the popovers. The food was some of the best I've ever eaten. The scenery was among the best I've ever been immersed in while eating. I savored every bite. I ate slowly. I completely enjoyed the experience.

This is the vision then—to eat as I ate at Jordon Pond every time I eat a meal. I will sit down (instead of standing at the sink). I will connect with whatever nature is available. I will eat slowly and savor each bite. I will only eat food that tastes good to me. Using this Jordon Pond experience, I am able to fully imagine and redefine myself.

Next I will engage the creative/meditative aspect of myself by writing, journaling, drawing, painting what that passion looks and feels like to me. As I said before in this writing, using an activity to engage the creative/meditative internal mode of being is the most crucial part, yet it is the one we least often take the time to purposefully engage. I am going to begin a painting this weekend that will embody this vision of savoring each morsel. However, the habit is so engrained in me that I will also do something before I eat anything that will invoke the feeling of savoring. I will take a moment to close my eyes and remember the Acadia dining experience, and I will ask myself to bring that feeling of savoring into the present moment while I dine.

Okay, so here is where the "rubber meets the road" as they say, and it's still me (Regina) speaking. Confessions of a lead foot! Now I have to take one of my non-green habits (gulp!) and take it through the steps so that I begin to turn it around. I hate to admit to this—it's embarrassing because I feel I ought to be green through and through. I traded my gas-hog car in—it was the best car I've ever driven in my life. I loved my Volvo AWD sport utility car. I could drive in any weather, on any terrain, and that car would go. I LOVED my Volvo.

But the deeper I got in to learning about sustainability, the more convinced I was that I had to trade the Volvo in on a car that was more fuel efficient. So I did. I bought a used Audi with a manual six speed transmission. It does a decent job on fuel use, averaging about 33 miles per gallon. (That's about twice what my Volvo was getting!) So, I improved, but of course, my standards are now higher and I think I ought to trade this car in on one that gets 60 or more miles per gallon.

Here's the truth about me as a driver—I have been in the habit of driving five miles an hour over the speed limit for as long as I can remember. Now, we all know that the faster we drive the more fuel we use, but driving is one of the things that I do without thinking about it. I'm not talking about quality of driving—I've not been in an accident since I was eighteen years old, and that is just over forty years ago. It's more like signing my name—the signature is legible and it's done with quality; however, I do it without thinking about it. I just sign my name.

In that same way, I just drive—I don't think about it. I just drive. So, why do I drive five miles an hour over the speed limit? I was thinking about that question as I drove in to work today. Speed is part of the equation, of course, and that is a value embedded in the Industrial Age worldview – the one I must extricate myself from. But there is also something about my valuing arrival at the destination more than the duration of the trip itself.

I thought to myself that if I extend that value to life, then what is the destination that I am rushing toward? It already feels like sixty years have gone by so quickly that it seems impossible! Why am I not valuing the trip—this moment? So this morning, I slowed down. I set the cruise control at the speed limit exactly and I consciously focused on noticing the drive itself. I noticed the deciduous trees turning their glorious fall colors. I noticed the Indiana corn and soybean fields—some harvested, others still standing. I noticed a hawk sitting on a utility line by the side of the road scouting for breakfast. I noticed the patches of greensward in the fields, and forested areas in the distance. I noticed that I was enjoying myself on this drive as I paid attention. Time elongated and I felt refreshed as I drove—a marked difference from the usual experience. I am determined to continue this practice and allow this way of driving to become my new habit.

Chapter 12:
Change-Making in the World

A crisis can be defined as a situation in which uncertainty is created because things are not working as planned or expected. We can experience crises on a personal as well as a societal level. From all we have said so far, there can be little doubt that we are experiencing a planetary crisis in relation to the sustainable systems of the earth. Below is the Chinese ideograph for the word "crisis." It is called *weiji*. The upper character, *wei*, means "danger." The lower character, *ji*, means "crucial turning point."

危
機

Centuries of cultural wisdom are distilled for us in these characters. Yes, a crisis presents a dangerous situation. Because previous patterns do not hold and there is much uncertainty, people can get hurt. But at the same time, a crisis can be a crucial turning point. Depending on how we understand the situation and the actions we choose to take, we can worsen the negative aspects of the crisis or we can rethink, recalculate, reorganize and move in a new direction. Thus a crisis, however unwelcome, presents us with an opportunity for growth and change. In response to the crisis, it is vital that we begin with our own personal transformation that will lead to social change and cultural evolution.

How can we take action ourselves, inspire others to take action, and as Gandhi says, be the change we wish to see in the world? We do what we can. Embracing the life we propose in this book is a call to personal transformation and to be leaders toward a new world view. We have talked in this book about additional qualities that we must take into account in order to create a sustainable life and society. Those qualities are Entropy, Time, and Nourishment, for both self and society.

We recognize that we can become aware of the change that is needed, yet do nothing to make that change happen. What can motivate us to take action? If we are in a burning building, our instincts of self-preservation kick in and we head for the exit and safety outside; however, if we're overcome by smoke before we're aware of the fire, we are rendered unable to save ourselves. Can we enlarge our ideas about "self-preservation" to include a more holistic vision of what "self" is?

Speaking of fire, making change—whether on a personal or a societal level—can be seen as equivalent to building a fire. The ability to start and sustain a fire is one of our oldest cultural assets, extending back to the Hunter-Gatherer Age. Other than language, there is probably no quality that sets us off more from other animal species. But fire, like the Chinese understanding of "crisis," is two sided. Out of control, fire can be incredibly destructive. On the other hand, the control of fire is arguably what made civilization possible.[85]

So how do you build and sustain a fire (or a personal or social change)? First you need fuel. That is, there must be a problem or a crisis that is combustible, that provides raw material. On a societal level, sociologists call this *structural conduciveness,* or a set of objective conditions that provide a basis for collective action.[86] In this book we have outlined the planet-wide crisis created by the thinking and practices of the Industrial Age. To overcome this crisis, we need to organize people into a broad-based social movement that can pressure institutions to change, from both inside—using existing levers of power—and from outside, using political pressure through the power of collective action.

Next in the fire-building process you must have tinder and a spark. The tinder is a general anxiety produced by a recognition that real conditions don't match our ideal expectations and a growing belief that a crisis looms. Sociologists call this *structural strain* and the *growth and spread of a generalized belief*. In the late Industrial Age we see countless examples of this: e.g., anxiety over rising fuel and energy prices, unease about potentially carcinogenic chemicals in our food, water, air, and household products, frustration with endless traffic jams, routinized and meaningless jobs, alienation from our neighbors, etc.[87]

The spark is an event that focuses this frustration and potentially provokes people to action. It is usually a dramatic event like a large power blackout, a massive oil spill, a series of hugely destructive hurricanes, a sensational crime that exposes the tenuous threads of community, or just a simple act that somehow captures the absurdity of the practices of the late Industrial Age. At any rate, people perceive the event as "the last straw," and are prepared to take action.

But just because people are prepared to take action doesn't mean they will. Catching the tinder on fire is not enough. In order to have a blazing fire, we must fan the flames and continue to stoke the fire. What this means for social action is that we must challenge and educate ourselves first, prior to the precipitating event. We must be ready with a new definition of the situation, a new and practical vision for the future, and a set of strategies for accomplishing needed change.

As we educate ourselves to the values and practices of The Green Age and connect with others who share our vision, we create the conditions for *mobilization for action,* in which a social movement comes together to create effective change. There are no guarantees, of course, but these are the necessary steps to building a fire that will not easily be quenched and will create lasting social change. See if you can see this process at work as Matt tells this story.

Matt's Story:

Nora, my daughter, and John are in their early 30's. They moved from the Midwest to Phoenix because of John's severe asthma and allergies. Nora is a teacher working with autistic and special needs children. John manages a company that produces neon signs. He is gradually establishing himself as a recognized glass artist. "I love glass," says John. "It is a renewable resource and I can make things out of recycled products."

They realize that in Phoenix they are living in one of the most unsustainable cities in the United States, but they try to do what they can to be green. They understand the importance of recycling. John and Nora share one car so they carpool to work. They are looking for a house close to public transportation. Nora says the growth of the Phoenix metropolitan area is essentially out of control. Every year thousands of acres of farm land and Sonoran desert are turned into suburban housing developments, strip malls and parking lots. It is one of those late 20th century endless suburbs where everyplace looks like everyplace else.

Phoenix is now the 6th largest metropolitan area in the US and has a population greater than 17 states. Phoenix is big—very big. It is also hot. Temperatures routinely exceed 110°F during the summer months. A normal summer day in Phoenix would certainly be a disaster in many other cities worldwide. What makes Phoenix habitable is simply mechanical air conditioning powered by electricity. The source of electricity in the Salt River Valley is hydroelectric generation.

Supply and demand of water has always been a concern in Phoenix, Arizona. Thus far, the state has avoided a water shortage of catastrophic proportions, and water use has been sufficient for the population's daily water needs. But with a growing population, a dwindling water supply, over a decade of drought, and the added perils of global warming, the pressure to solve the water issue grows stronger each year. This past summer people were strongly encouraged to take personal initiative to conserve their daily water usage.

One day on the way to work Nora and John stopped to get gas. While John was filling the tank Nora dashed across the street to use the restroom at McDonalds. "I couldn't believe what I saw," she said. "There, standing in the parking lot, was an employee watering the blacktop! I mean just standing there with a hose pouring water on the ground like you would water your lawn." When Nora approached the attendant she discovered that this was his daily duty and a policy of the restaurant. "I thought I was going crazy." She said. "How could this happen when we were supposedly having a water shortage?" The Manager just shrugged. "It's corporate policy," he said.

The support group is the central methodology of all successful Twelve Step programs. For those who are serious about change, success can be found by locating others who have the same goals. Benjamin Franklin stands as a guiding light for the power of developing a mutually supporting "self-help" group. Essentially self educated, Franklin describes his methods for self improvement in his famous autobiography.[88] As a young man in Philadelphia he organized meetings with others so that they could help each other improve their writing and speaking skills.

In 1727, Benjamin Franklin created the Junto, a group of "like minded aspiring artisans and tradesmen who hoped to improve themselves while they improved their community." The Junto was a discussion group for issues of the day; it subsequently gave rise to many organizations in Philadelphia.

Reading was a great pastime of the Junto, but books were rare and expensive. The members created a library, and initially pooled their own books together, which led to Franklin's idea of establishing the subscription library – the first in the American colonies.

Email, Facebook, and Twitter, is the 21st century answer to Franklin's Junta. When Nora got to her computer she reported her experience of seeing the attendant watering the parking lot on her Facebook page and e-mailed friends around the country. This turned into a group effort to find out if blacktop watering was a common occurrence. The result? Nora discovered that it is a common policy for fast food restaurants to wash down their parking lots daily!

Nora was shocked and depressed by this news and the magnitude of the problem. She was also frustrated and stymied. Opportunity presented itself one month later. University of Arizona professor Robert Glennon was scheduled for an interview on National Public Radio to discuss his book: *Unquenchable: America's Water Crisis and What To Do About It.* Nora saw this as a chance to get the message out and speak to a professional on how to combat this massive misuse of water.

During the question and answer portion of the segment, Nora was put on the radio and explained what she had seen and the results of her research. Professor Glennon was shocked by this information and declared Nora a "Steward of the Planet" for spreading the news. Have fast food restaurants stopped watering their driveways? Probably not yet. But Nora made the effort to speak out and now millions of radio listeners also know about the strange practice of driveway watering. Who else will speak out because of what they heard on the radio?

More importantly, who will begin and sustain conversations with their friends and neighbors about these important topics?

As Meg Wheatley notes, "Human conversation is the most ancient and easiest way to cultivate the conditions for change—personal change, community and organizational change, planetary change."[89] It works because conversation is a fundamentally social and connective process. When talking about important topics and really listening to one another, people become vulnerable and reinforce social bonds. They also access a collective wisdom not otherwise available.

Juanita Brown reminds us that social revolutions have always begun with conversations—from the salons of Paris prior to the French Revolution, to the discussions on college campuses that led to the Freedom Riders, to the consciousness-raising groups of the women's movement. Brown and her colleagues call the collective wisdom of the group "collaborative intelligence," and have developed a process to focus conversations.[90] The goal, she says, is to have "generative conversations" to create "actionable knowledge."

This is accomplished through a focused, iterative process that they call The World Café. People sit together and discuss a topic in small groups, then rotate to another group so that everyone eventually talks with everyone else. Key ideas are written on post-it notes, which are placed on a wall for collective viewing and evaluation. More conversation ensues as action strategies are honed. Whether using this focused process or simply sharing together in dorm rooms, apartments, homes, parks, churches, break rooms, and classrooms, the structure of

The Green Age and the strategies to bring it into existence will surely be honed by conversation. And that conversation doesn't necessarily have to be face-to-face. Anthony Weston notes that, using the internet, "we could create a *truly* 'new world order', starting right now, out of virtual person-to-person dialogue around the globe."[91]

We will all be frustrated if we expect big, immediate changes. But small actions can eventually have dynamic results.

Remember – it only takes a small spark to make a blazing fire. Can you, as Gandhi said, "be the change you wish to see in the world"? A common joke in the Midwestern United States where we live is that if you don't like the weather just wait a few minutes and it will change. This is a humorous recognition that weather is difficult to predict beyond the broader seasonal norms based on long term statistics.

The reason that weather is difficult to predict is that very small events can have enormous effect on weather transformations. This has been termed the "Butterfly Effect" and encapsulates the more technical notion of sensitive dependence on initial conditions in chaos theory. The idea is that small variations impacting a system may produce large variations in the long term behavior of the system. The initial work in this area was produced by Edward Norton Lorenz, a mathematician and meteorologist. Norton was studying the predictability of the weather. In 1961, he was using a numerical computer model to rerun a weather prediction when, as a shortcut on a number in the sequence, he entered the decimal .506 instead of entering the full .506127 that the computer would hold. The result was a completely different weather scenario!

The implications are profound. Lorenz realized that the flip of a butterfly's wing might create tiny changes in the atmosphere that could ultimately alter the path of a tornado or delay, accelerate, or even prevent the occurrence of a hurricane. The flapping wing represents a small change in the initial condition of the system, which causes a chain of events leading to large-scale alterations of events. Had the butterfly not flapped its wings, the trajectory of the system might have been vastly different.

What does this mean for us? As part of an interconnected global system, each action we take, no matter how small, sets in motion events of which we have no ken. Collectively, our power will act as a blasting force of butterfly wings that could change the course of the future. "Never doubt," said pioneering anthropologist Margaret Mead, "that a small group of thoughtful, committed citizens can change the world. Indeed, it is the only thing that ever has."

Malcolm Gladwell makes this point in his bestseller *The Tipping Point*.[92] Gladwell suggests that social change is viral. That is, new ideas, practices, ways of thinking are potentially contagious. They can spread through a society much like a viral epidemic – quickly and dramatically, once they catch hold. We have long known that violence, negativity, and cynicism are viral phenomena. Many global conflicts that seem intractable are the result of a spiral of escalating violent acts by each side. No doubt you are familiar with the "broken window syndrome." A building can stand empty, neglected, but intact for a period of time. But once someone breaks a single window, every single other window is broken in short order. The building has become "fair game."

But, says William Ury, "Violence is not the only contagious phenomenon. So is cooperation."[93] This is illustrated by the Random Acts of Kindness movement. The idea is to do something nice for someone else, even a complete stranger. Moved by a gift of compassion, that person will do something nice for someone else, and so on. In the movie *Pay It Forward,* a young schoolboy develops a project to encourage people to engage in acts of kindness without any expectation of something in return. The idea becomes contagious and goes viral. A recent television commercial illustrated this as well, with strangers on urban streets performing acts of kindness for one another after witnessing similar behavior by someone else.

When it comes to social change, says Gladwell, little changes can have big effects. Like the wings of a butterfly changing the weather. How does this happen, and how, specifically can it happen to usher in The Green Age? Echoing Margaret Mead, Gladwell describes what he calls The Law of the Few. When we trace the origin of fads, fashions, or new ideas, we find that just a relative handful of people are responsible for their origin, growth and spread. These pioneers and early adopters are at key nodes of social networks, and are thus in a position to disproportionately influence others. This "Law of the Few," Gladwell observes, "says that there are exceptional people out there who are capable of starting epidemics. All you have to do is find them."[94]

So one important strategy is to identify these influentials and educate them about the problems of The Industrial Age and the promise of The Green Age. But this is not the only strategy. Gladwell also states that "small, close-knit groups have the power to magnify the epidemic potential of a message or idea."[95] So processes of democratic dialogue, like The World Café discussed earlier, and the use of new social media provide alternative pathways for the idea of The Green Age to "go viral."

At bottom, of course, people will only be spurred to action by ideas that seem vital and moving, that tap into deep feelings and associations. Gladwell calls this the quality of "stickiness." Is the message memorable? Does it "grab" people and make them pay attention? Does it "stick"? Certainly that first picture of the earth taken from space was such an event. It was a consciousness-changer for many people.

We hope that the ideas that we have laid out in this book have the quality of stickiness, and that they will prompt people to sustained action. After all, as Anthony Weston observes, "the single greatest contributor to sustained creativity—after a few methods, anyway—is *persistence*.[96] But we also know that it is by talking together, educating ourselves and each other, and working together that we will usher in The Green Age.

Together, let us begin.

ABOUT THE AUTHORS

Regina Leffers, Ph.D. is an author, speaker, and artist, living in Pentwater, Michigan. She earned her doctoral degree in Philosophy from Purdue University. While she was writing her dissertation, Regina helped her brother start and build his construction company. In the 1990' she started her own construction company which specialized in sustainable construction—a method of building which uses less energy to heat or cool the structure. Regina recently retired from the position of Director of the IPFW Center of Excellence for the Built Environment and professor of Sustainable Construction. She is a founding member and past President of the Northeast Indiana Green Build Coalition, and was Co-Chair of Mayor Graham Richard's Green Ribbon Commission for the City of Fort Wayne, Indiana. Her textbook, *Sustainable Construction and Design*, published by Pearson/Prentice Hall, is widely used. Regina has conducted numerous design charettes, a process of problem-solving in which stakeholders work together to craft solutions that address all connected aspects of the environment in which the problem is embedded. You can contact her by e-mail at Regina@createthegreenage.com.

Matthew Kubik is an author, speaker, educator, architect, and artist living in Michigan City, Indiana. He holds a professional degree in architecture from the University of Notre Dame. In London, England he did post-graduate studies at the the Royal College of Art and is a 1977 graduate of the Architectural Association School of Architecture. Matt earned a Graduate Diploma (M.Arch equivalent) for his modeling of community energy use and energy conservation research. He has won awards for Excellence in Architecture granted by the American Institute of Architects. Since the 1970's Matt has designed projects striving for minimum environmental impact. Matt has lectured internationally on sustainable urban planning, architecture and interior design. In 2009 he served as consultant to the History Channel for *Life After People—The Series* regarding the entropic decay of the Chicago urban environment. You can contact Matt by e-mail at Matt@createthegreenage.com.

Patrick J. Ashton, Ph.D. is an author, speaker, professor, and mediator living in Fort Wayne, Indiana. He is an associate professor of Sociology and Director of Peace and Conflict Studies at Indiana University Purdue University Fort Wayne. Pat earned a B.A. in Sociology from Oakland University and a M.A. and Ph.D. in Sociology from Michigan State University. He is a certified community mediator and mediation trainer and helped to develop and run a free community mediation service. Pat's research and writing focus has centered on the interface of human community and the built environment for over 30 years. His publications include development of a paradigm for sustainability in the built environment, analyses of the political economy of suburban development, the impact of a large-scale plant closing on an urban community, and the characteristics and dynamics of community organization. In 1999 Pat, along with Matt Kubik, produced and presented a 1-hour live program, "Urbanism Run Amok: Can the City Be Saved in the Next Millennium?" broadcast to 92 college campuses by the National Collegiate Honors Council Satellite Seminar Program. Recently Pat has conducted sustainable design workshops in the United States and Europe. You can contact Pat by e-mail at Pat@createthegreenage.com.

Endnotes

[1] Joseph Campbell, *The Hero with a Thousand Faces*, Princeton, NJ: Princeton University Press, 1968, p. 11

[2] Robert N. Bellah, Richard Madsen, William M. Sullivan, Ann Swidler, and Steven M. Tipton, *Habits of the Heart: Individualism and Commitment in American Life.* Berkeley: University of California Press, 1985, p. 275.

[3] See the analysis of female fertility figurines at arthistoryresources.net/willendorf/willendorfwoman.html

[4] See, for example, Riane Eisler, *The Chalice and The Blade: Our History, Our Future.* San Francisco: Harper Collins, 1987.

[5] William Ury, *The Third Side: Why We Fight and How We Can Stop.* Penguin Books, 2000, pp. 73-4.

[6] For a discussion of the origin of the industrial factory as a system of social control, see Stephen A. Marglin, "What Do Bosses Do? The Origin and Functions of Hierarchy in Capitalist Production," *Review of Radical Political Economics* 6 (Summer 1974).

[7] The Gaia Theory was first proposed by chemist James Lovelock in the 1970s. It sees the Earth as a single complex, self-regulating system. See James Lovelock, *The Ages of Gaia: A Biography of Our Living Earth.* New York: Norton, 1995; and James Lovelock, *The Vanishing Face of Gaia: A Final Warning.* New York: Basic Books, 2009.

[8] For a manifesto of this vision, see Riane Eisler, *The Real Wealth of Nations: Creating a Caring Economics*. San Francisco: Berrett-Koehler, 2007.

[9] Henryk Skolimowski, *The Participatory Mind.* London: Arkana, 1994.

[10] See Francis Bacon, *The New Organon, or True Directions Concerning the Interpretation of Nature.* 1620. Available at www.constitution.org/bacon/nov_org.htm

[11] René Descartes, *Meditations on First Philosophy.* New York: Cambridge University Press, 1986, p.67.

[12] See www.grc.nasa.gov/WWW/k-12/airplane/newton.html

[13] John Locke, *Two Treatises of Government.* New Haven, CT: Yale University Press, 2003,

[14] Adam Smith, *An Inquiry into the Nature and Causes of the Wealth of Nations.* New York: Modern Library, 1994.

[15] Patrick J. Ashton and Matthew Kubik, "The Berlin Manifesto: Social Transformation for Sustainable Design." *Design Principles and Practices: An International Journal* 3:6, 2009, pp. 281-289. We are indebted in this analysis to Jeremy Rifkin, *Entropy, A New World View,* New York: Viking Press, 1980.

[16] Quote found at www.earthportal.org/?p=82

[17] See www.humanthermodynamics.com/clausius.html

[18] Rifkin, *op. cit,* pg 35.

[19] Chart found at www.globalization101.org/issue_sub/energy/energyappendies/Peak_theory#

[20] Paul Krugman, "The Goldbug Variations" Available at www.pkarchive.org/cranks/goldbug.html

[21] Krugman, *ibid.*

[22] Krugman, *ibid.*

23 Krugman, *ibid.*

24 M. King Hubbert included this idea in his 1974 address to Congress on the Nature of Growth. In National Energy Conservation Policy Act of 1974, hearings before the Subcommittee on the Environment, U.S. House Committee on Interior and Insular Affairs, Subcommittee on the Environment, 93rd Congress, 2nd Session, June 6, 1974, pp. 51-78. Serial No. 93-55. Washington: U.S. Government Printing Office, 1974.

25 Bob Dylan, "The Times They Are A-changin" Lyrics available at www.metrolyrics.com/the-times-they-are-achangin-lyrics-bob-dylan.html

26 M. Regina Leffers, *Sustainable Construction and Design.* Columbus, OH: Pearson-Prentice Hall, 2009, p. 30.

27 See Max Weber, *The Protestant Ethic and the Spirit of Capitalism.* New York: Scribner, 1958.

28 George Ritzer, *The McDonaldization of Society, revised New Century Edition.* Thousand Oaks, CA: Pine Forge Press, 2004.

29 George Ritzer, *Enchanting a Disenchanted World: Revolutionizing the Means of Consumption, Second Edition.* Thousand Oaks, CA: Pine Forge Press, 2005.

30 Thomas L. Friedman, *Hot, Flat, and Crowded: Why We Need a Green Revolution—and How it Can Renew America. Release 2.0.* New York: Picador, 2009, p. 7.

31 Bacon, *op. cit.*

32 Quote available at http://en.wikipedia.org/wiki/General_Electric_Theater

[33] Donella H. Meadows, Dennis L. Meadows, Jørgen Randers, and William W. Behrens III, *The Limits to Growth*. Universe Books, 1972.

[34] Vice President Richard Cheney, "Remarks regarding energy policy" at the Annual Meeting of the Associated Press in Toronto, Canada, April 30, 2001. Available at www.pbs.org/newshour/bb/environment/energy/cheney_4-30.html

[35] Peter Reason and Hilary Bradbury, editors, *Handbook of action research: Participative Inquiry and Practice*.. Thousand Oaks, CA: Sage Publications, 1998.

[36] This quote is taken from a talk given at the Architectural Association Forum (London) on Thursday June 20 (1974), by Professor Henryk Skolimowski of the Humanities Dept, College of Engineering, Ann Arbor, Michigan.

[37] *ibid.*

[38] Illustrations by Matthew Kubik.

[39] Proportion study by Matthew Kubik based on Leonardo da Vinci's anatomic drawing of the lungs and circulatory system.

[40] www4.ncsu.edu/~nwsfo/storage/cases/20030918

[41] Gemini Observatory Image/GMOS Commissioning Team/AURA

[42] www.dailyyonder.com/presidency-obamas-genes

[43] Rohde, DLT; Olson S, Chang JT (2004). "Modeling the recent common ancestry of all living humans." *Nature* **431**: 562–566.

44 John Guare, *Six Degrees of Separation: A Play*. New York: Random House, 1990.

45 www.guardian.co.uk/technology/2008/aug/03/internet.email

46 Parliament of the World's Religions, "Declaration Toward a Global Ethic," Chicago, Illinois, USA, 4 September 1993.

47 *The Tale of the Eloquent Peasant*, 109 - 110 Translated by R.B. Parkinson. The original dates to 1640 BCE and may be the earliest version ever written.

48 Socrates (436-338 BCE)

49 Seneca the Younger, *Epistulae morales ad Lucilium* 47:11

50 *Leviticus* 9:18

51 *The Mahabharata*, one of the two major Sanskrit epics of ancient India.

52 Number 13 of Imam "Al-Nawawi's Forty Hadiths."

53 *New Testament*, Matthew 5:43; 19:19; 22:39; Mark 12:31; Romans 13:9; Galatians 5:14; James 2:8; Luke 10:27

54 Jensen, Peter S., Mrazek, David, Knapp, Penelope K., Steinberg, Laurence, Pfeffer, Cynthia, Schowalter, John, & Shapiro, Theodore. (Dec 1997) "Evolution and revolution in child psychiatry: ADHD as a disorder of adaptation. (attention-deficit hyperactivity syndrome)." *Journal of the American Academy of Child and Adolescent Psychiatry*. 36. p. 1672. (10). July 14 2007.

55 Buckminster Fuller [1970] 1983. *Intuition, second edition*. San Luis Obispo, CA: Impact Publishers.

56 D. Bohm & B. Hiley. "On the Intuitive Understanding of Nonlocality as Implied by Quantum Theory," *Foundations of Physics*, vol. 5 (1975), pp.96, 102.

57 David Bohm. *Wholeness and the Implicate Order* London: Ark, 1983, p.174.

58 Candace Pert, *Molecules of Emotion* New York: Simon & Schuster, 1999.

59 Image available at apod.nasa.gov/apod/ap070325.htm

60 This description of the physical structure of matter beginning with the Buckminster Fuller quote was first published in the textbook: *Sustainable Construction and Design*, by Regina Leffers. New York: Prentice Hall, 2009.

61 Mitchell, *op. cit.*

62 Following current scientific practice, BCE stands for Before the Current Era, and CE stands for the Current Era.

63 Sim van der Ryn and Stuart Cowan, *Ecological Design.* Washington, D.C.: Island Press, 1996, p. x.

64 *ibid.,* p. ix.

65 E.F. Schumacher, *Small is Beautiful—Economics as If People Mattered.* London: Blond & Briggs Ltd., 1973.

66 John C. Bogle, *Enough: True Measures of Money, Business, and Life.* New York: Wiley, 2010.

67 Schumacher, *op. cit.*

68 Schumacher, *op. cit.*

[69] Ury, *op. cit.*, p. 109.

[70] Van der Ryn and Cowan, *op. cit.*, p. 66.

[71] Winifred Gallagher, *The Power of Place: How Our Surroundings Shape Our Thoughts, Emotions, and Actions.* New York: Poseidon Press, 1993, p. 228.

[72] David W. Orr, *Earth in Mind: On Education, Environment, and the Human Prospect. 10th Anniversary Edition.* Washington: Island Press, 2004, p. 5.

[73] John Elkington, "Towards the Sustainable Corporation: Win-Win-Win Business Strategies for Sustainable Development," *California Management Review* 36, no. 2 (1994): 90–100.

[74] Sustainability Reporting Guidelines, Version 3.0, Global Reporting Initiative. The guidelines can be downloaded for free from their website: www.globalreporting.org.

[75] *ibid.,* pg. 29.

[76] Bellah et al., *op. cit.*, p. 282.

[77] Edgar D. Mitchell, wrote *A Parody on Sustainability* in 1996. You can read the essay in its entirety at: www.edmitchellapollo14.com/go_forth_and_sustain_the_world.htm

[78] Friedman, *op. cit.*, pp. 8-9.

[79] Elisabeth Kübler-Ross, *On Death and Dying.* London: Routledge, 1969.

[80] David J. Schwartz, *The Magic of Thinking Big.* New York: Cornerstone Books, 1965.

[81] In the United States there are 1000 real calories in one food calorie, so a U.S. food calorie is actually a kilocalorie. A real calorie is the heat required to raise the temperature 1 gram of water 1 degree Celsius. In Europe food is labeled in kilocalories.

[82] See, for example, William McDonough and Michael Braungart, *Cradle to Cradle: Remaking the Way We Make Things*. New York: North Point Press, 2002.

[83] www.brainandhealth.com/Brain-Waves.html

[84] The illustration is from geraldguild.com/blog/2011/02/18/brain-waves-and-other-brain-measures

[85] We are indebted to MacBeth and Fine for this metaphor, though they use it primarily to analyze conflict. See Fiona MacBeth and Nic Fine, *Playing with Fire: Creative Conflict Resolution for Young Adults*. Gabriola Island, British Columbia: New Society Publishers, 1995.

[86] For the conditions necessary to create a social movement, see Neil J. Smelser, *Theory of Collective Behavior*. New York: The Free Press, 1963. For rules for solving social problems, see Clayton A. Hartjen, *Possible Trouble: An Analysis of Social Problems*. New York: Praeger, 1977.

[87] For instance, sociologist Riley Dunlap found that public awareness of the seriousness of environmental problems and support for regulations to protect the environment increased dramatically between the late 1960s and the early 1990s. Riley E. Dunlap, "Trends in Public Opinion Toward Environmental Issues: 1965-1990" pp. 89-113 in Riley E. Dunlap and Angela E. Mertig, eds., *American Environmentalism: The U.S. Environmental Movement, 1970-1990*. New York: Taylor and Francis, 1992.

[88] Benjamin Franklin, *Autobiography*.
www.gutenberg.org/ebooks/20203

[89] Meg Wheatley, *Turning to One Another, 2nd edition.* San Francisco, CA: Berrett-Koehler Publishers, 2009, p. 7.

[90] Juanita Brown, *The World Café: Shaping Our Futures Through Conversations That Matter.* San Francisco, CA: Berrett-Koehler Publishers, 2005.

[91] Anthony Weston, *How to Re-Imagine the World: A Pocket Guide for Practical Visionaries.* Gabriola Island, BC, Canada: New Society Publishers, 2007, p. 3.

[92] Malcolm Gladwell, *The Tipping Point: How Little Things Can Make a Big Difference.* New York: Back Bay Books, 2002.

[93] Ury, *op. cit.*, p. 13

[94] Gladwell, *op. cit.,* p. 132

[95] Gladwell, *op. cit.*, p. 174

[96] Weston, *op. cit.*, p. 49.

Share your story!

If you were moved, provoked, and/or inspired by what you read in this book, or if you have a story of your own about transforming your life for sustainability we'd love to hear from you. Log on to our book website below and share your story with other Green Agents of sustainable change.

www.thegreenagebook.com